The
Ultimate Victory

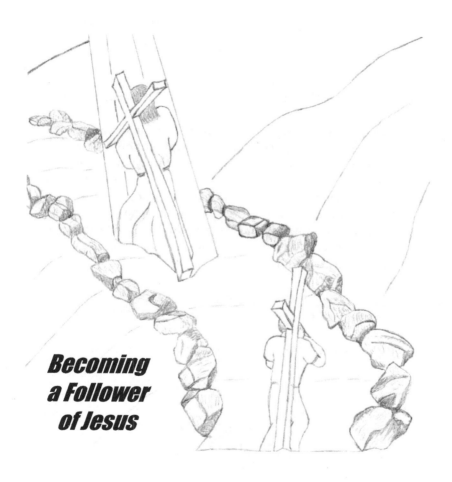

Becoming
a Follower
of Jesus

Dr. James B. Joseph
"Brother James"

The Ultimate Victory
Becoming a Follower of Jesus

DR. JAMES B. JOSEPH | "BROTHER JAMES"

ISBN: 979-8-9884593-1-6
Library of Congress Control Number: 2023910021

Author's Website: www.injesusservice.com

Pfafftown, NC USA

**"Your Word is a lamp to my feet,
indeed, a light to my pathway!"
Psalm 119:105**

**Through the guidance
of the Father
and help of the Holy Spirit,
let's follow Jesus closely!**

Foreword

Everyone is loved by God more than any can imagine! As you journey through *The Ultimate Victory: Becoming a Follower of Jesus*, the experience should help you understand God and His Creation more fully highlighting His great love for you and His desired place for you in His eternal family resulting in a deepened personal relationship with Him. You are wonderfully made to have a nature like God Himself, but only if you allow Him to guide you into becoming a mature loving righteous person. Throughout the Creation process starting with Adam, God works continually bringing spiritual enlightenment, love, joy, and internal peace to all who listen to Him.

When one allows God to teach them how to love Him and others and truly starts trusting His leadership, He then places them into His eternal close loving righteous family.[1] *This is described by Jesus as being "born again,"*[2] *which is the ultimate victory for any human being.* This ultimate victory includes godly empowerment for Jesus' followers helping them to experience more and more of His joy while carrying out their personal assignments. It sounds easy, but it is not! It is much easier to stay on the commonly shared life path that is traveled by most people ignoring God and His leading.

This book has been written to help everyone know God better. Reading through it should help you realize more fully what God is asking of each of us and what Satan is doing to quench the leading of the Holy Spirit. Following Jesus more faithfully into ongoing spiritual warfare will help free you from this world's bondage. In the process, you will experience more of Jesus' joy as you help others come to know God and His great desire for them to be part of His eternal holy family, the Crown Jewel of His Creation. Let's not miss out on the best that our Heavenly Father has for each of us and forfeit the love, joy, inner peace, and excitement that come with faithfully following Jesus!

– In Jesus' Service, Brother James

Bible Book Abbreviations Used & Important Notes

Old Testament

Genesis: Gen
Exodus: Exod
Leviticus: Lev
Numbers: Num
Deuteronomy: Deut
Joshua: Josh
Judges: Judg
1-2 Samuel: 1-2 Sam
1-2 Chronicles: 1-2 Chr
Nehemiah: Neh
Esther: Esth
Psalms: Ps
Proverbs: Prov
Ecclesiastes: Eccl
Isaiah: Isa
Jeremiah: Jer
Lamentations: Lam
Ezekiel: Ezek
Daniel: Dan
Hosea: Hos
Obadiah: Obad
Micah: Mic
Nahum: Nah
Habakkuk: Hab
Zephaniah: Zeph
Haggai: Hag
Zechariah: Zech
Malachi: Mal

Bible Translations

In this book, the Bible translations are the author's.

New Testament

Matthew: Matt
Romans: Rom
1-2 Corinthians: 1-2 Cor
Galatians: Gal
Ephesians: Eph
Philippians: Phil
Colossians: Col
1-2 Thessalonians: 1-2 Thess
1-2 Timothy: 1-2 Tim
Philemon: Phlm
Hebrews: Heb
James: Jas
1-2 Peter: 1-2 Pet
Revelation: Rev

Important Notice:

The author has included some important Greek New Testament and Hebrew Old Testament words in *italics* within parenthesis throughout this book for those of you who like in-depth understanding. If you do not have reference books for Greek and Hebrew, do a Google search for each word of interest.

Example Search: "meaning of the Greek word *dei*"

Extended Table of Contents

Extended Table of Contents

1

Understanding God's Creation
through Its Completion

God is awesome in every way including His phenomenal loving-kindness! Following God and His way of life produces the best outcome for all people of all time. Let's consider carefully the outcome of His grand creative design. Not only does He have the final say in everything (sovereignty), He is extremely capable and does not make mistakes! Before He physically implemented His Creation, He knew how everyone throughout the Creation would respond to Him and His perfect way of life throughout their physical lives and what His response would be for each.[(a)] As a key part of the Creation, the Father sent His Son, Jesus, the promised Messiah, at just the right time[(b)] to save all people of all time who would learn to love, trust, and obey Them.

The Father, Son, and Holy Spirit created humanity to live in peace and harmony with Them and one another experiencing great joy.[3] So what happened? It can be seen in God's Word that He wants to interact closely with each person, so why so much bad behavior, disharmony, chaos, and pain? The key to this temporary suffering originates from God's desire to add abundantly free beings to His family. The Father, Son, and Holy Spirit **did not want robots** to join their close eternal family, but instead individuals who would consider joining Them because of Their loving-kindness and righteous way of life. They wanted highly interactive freewill beings voluntarily wanting to live with them in a mature mutual caring relationship. Knowing that this abundant freedom would result temporarily in great sin, which at times would produce great pain, sorrow, and disharmony, They worked out a plan that actually removes all bad actions (sin) from those

---

a: (a) Rom 8:28-30; Eph 1:3-8; 1 Peter 1:1-2; (b) Gal 4:4.

who learn to return Their love producing a sinless eternal family. Anything less than an eternal freewill sinless family at the end of the Creation would produce an eternal holy family that would still experience some level of sorrow and pain.[a] This was unacceptable to Them.

Some may question this creative approach, but keep in mind that this abundant freedom with its resulting pain, hurt, and sorrow throughout the Creation shows the importance that God places on creating a freewill eternal family. God is willing to allow some very hurtful actions throughout the Creation along with the majority of His children rejecting His leadership in order to have a freewill family with everyone having His moral nature.

Have you ever considered how much free will you actually have? It seems that you have a fair amount of freedom regarding everyday life, but even that seems to be partly controlled by a steady stream of events over which you have little or no control such as what others do, the weather, or even some parts of your own health. What about current issues such as finding long lasting inner peace and joy? What about the eternal issue of living with God forever in perfect love, peace, and joy versus being separated from Him forever to live in constant unrest and chaos?

I want you to know up-front, that our Heavenly Father loves you beyond what you can presently comprehend and wants you to want to get to know Him well[b] and then receive Him into your life as the loving father that He is.[c] If that becomes your desire, you will come to a place where you want Him and His Son, Jesus, to guide you (lordship). It is important to keep in mind that God's greatest desire and joy through His Creation is for as many as are willing to receive Him into their lives returning His love and accepting His lordship.[4] [d]

God's Desired Intimacy Should Bring Joy

Does God seem too distant, righteous, and glorious to want a close relationship with you? Because of our sin, it is

---

a: (a) Rev 21:1-4; cf. Rom 8:16-23; (b) Matt 22:37; (c) Deut 30:19-20; (d) Rom 8:28; cf. James 1:12; 2:5; and others.

normally easier to contemplate a distant relationship with God instead of allowing God to teach us that He actually wants to live with us in a close relationship. It seems that if we get too close to God, our sin will tarnish His reputation and glory. But, just the opposite is true: God's willingness to work with us in our sinful and sometimes hostile state shows His true nature of pure loving-kindness that is demonstrated through His justice tempered with mercy and grace.[a] In fact, not only did Jesus come into our world as a worker born in an animal shelter instead of as a king born in a palace, His ministry of teaching and miracles were aimed at *all* including the greatest leaders to the least influential. Because of His willingness to associate with flagrant sinners, His reputation seemed to have been tarnished by some who did not understand how godly love works to lift all.[b] But, in the end, God's glorious nature based on impartial loving-kindness, grace, and truth will be clearly seen by everyone.[c]

Have you ever had quiet moments when God seemed so close that you were overwhelmed with joy? Have you come to a place in life that you are experiencing God's love, joy, and inner peace at least occasionally? If not, it may be that you have been too busy, which has resulted in blocking much of God's self-revelation for you. If Satan can keep people busy and reduce or eliminate their consideration of God and His desired eternal close loving righteous family, he is accomplishing much in his fight against God.

During this part of the Creation, the path to greater joy and inner peace starts with *listening* to the One who is personally developing you, your Heavenly Father.[d] This is the same one who wants an intimate relationship with you. One of the many ways of listening to God is by reading His Word daily and receiving it into your mind and heart. Through His Word, you discover that as you become more willing to do His will, He helps you more fully understand His Word.[e]

If you have not personally been experiencing any excitement, joy, and inner peace in your walk with Jesus, you should. Even if you think that you are not worthy to experience such joy, you are worthy through Jesus Christ and His redeeming

---

a: (a) Rom 5:8-10; (b) Matt 9:9-13; 11:18-19; cf. Luke 15:32; (c) Rev 22:5; Phil 2:5-11; 3:20-21; (d) John 15:2; (e) John 7:17.

death. Jesus helps all of His true followers experience an inner peace and joy that can ultimately only come from Our Heavenly Father, a peace and joy that is grounded in godly love demonstrating concern for all.

If you are willing to do the Father's will, His Word will teach you reality [a] and start transforming you into His image.[b] You will join Him in rescuing those who will listen from some of this present-day's worldly pain and future eternal suffering and shame.

Although Jesus dreaded the Cross,[c] His joy became full when He knew that the time had come for Him to die providing salvation (complete sin removal) for all who would receive God into their lives.[d] He knew that His death would provide a miraculous removal of sin and a righteous transformation for all people of all time who obediently listen to His heavenly Father. *There is no greater joy that you will ever experience than when helping those whom you love see a need to ask God for help in changing from a present life of ongoing sin to a present and future life of eternal godly loving-kindness, righteousness, grace, and truth.*[5] [e] As God teaches you to love others more, consider the joy of helping others know God more fully. The overall context of Scripture clearly shows that "God is love," and that He wants all to come to repentance (turning from self-centeredness to Him and His way of life) joining His eternal loving mutually-interactive close-knit righteous family.[f]

You Can Trust What Jesus Said

If you question the validity of Jesus' claim to be the Son of God, who came to teach everyone reality (truth)[6] and die on everyone's behalf in order to remove individual bad behavior (sin) from those who receive God into their lives as lord and savior,[g]

---

a: (a) John 7:17; 8:31-32;18:37; (b) 1 John 3:11-18; (c) Matt 26:36-46; Luke 22:39-46; (d) John 17:13; Heb 12:1-2; (e) John 1:14; 15:8-11; (f) 1 John 4:16; 1 Peter 3:9; John 3:14-17; and others; (g) Col 2:13-14; 2 Cor 5:21; 1 Peter 2:24;

let's consider the main point that proves that Jesus' teachings are true. *What He has taught us through His disciples' writings has been verified by the details of history.* After Jesus was crucified, He was raised from the dead, which proclaims the reality of what God had already foretold to earlier generations (prophecy) and what Jesus proclaimed in His ministry.[a] With Jesus' resurrection being verifiable, it follows logically that what He said during His ministry including what He said about His upcoming death and resurrection[b] are all true, which includes the fact that the Father desires everyone to have an opportunity to have the same unity and love with Him that Jesus has.[c]

If you are wondering about the overall validity of what is written in the New Testament including what Jesus taught, let's consider a few facts: (1) Matthew and John were written by close student-followers (disciples) of Jesus who worked with Him throughout His ministry years and saw Him after His resurrection.[d] Luke was written by a physician who carefully investigated Jesus' ministry, death, and resurrection seeking accuracy,[e] and Mark was written by a close student-follower of Peter; (2) some of the New Testament letters were written by John, Peter, James, and Jude who learned from Jesus personally including during His forty days of teaching after His resurrection;[f] (3) one of the letter was written by the unknown writer of Hebrews who understood well the importance of having a sinless High Priest; and (4) multiple letters were written by Paul, who became an ideal witness because he was a young religious student who knew the Old Testament writings well and initially wanted to destroy Jesus' followers until the resurrected Jesus personally revealed Himself to him as the true Messiah fulfilling Scripture.[f]

Keep in mind that the majority of the New Testament letters were written approximately 20-35 years after Jesus' death and resurrection, and therefore, many people who had personally

---

a: (a) Ps 16:10; 1 Cor 15:3-8; Matt 26:2, 60-61; 27:39-40; John 2:19-22; (b) John 2:19-22; Matt 16:21; Luke 24:6-8; (c) John 15:10; 17:20-23; (d) 1 John 1:1-3; (f) Luke 1:1-4; (e) Acts 1:1-3; (f) Gal 1:11-24; Acts 22:1-22; 23:6.

seen and heard Jesus during His ministry, death, and resurrection period were still alive. *Consider the fact that the details within these letters were all verifiable at the time of their writings, and if there had been misinformation within them, the bad information would have hurt the writers' and Church's credibility as it proclaimed the Good News of what God was doing. Any bad information at that time would have hindered the Gospel message instead of helping it spread like wildfire. Therefore, we can count on the overall historical accuracy of what these writers said within their letters.*

And even though the final form of the written Gospel presentations were completed at various times throughout the first century, the core of all Gospel presentations was based on Jesus' teaching and ministry and was already being proclaimed shortly after Jesus' resurrection.[a]

Design in General

Prior to delving into some of the key elements of God's very complex Creation to begin to understand how awesome He really is, let's consider a few straightforward creations that God has helped mankind with that have a fair degree of accuracy and success.

First, consider something as straightforward as building homes. There are thousands of people all over the world who are competent to design, secure materials, and then assemble quality homes. Then, consider something more complex like building airplanes for various usages. After the basic elements of flying were figured out at the turn of the twentieth century by Orville and Wilbur Wright, who successfully figured out a good navigational control system and a wing design,[7] man has been designing all types of aircraft with different usages in mind and is able to order or manufacture the needed parts and then assemble the planes with a high degree of accuracy and success. We could go on and discuss more complex designs such as space stations and space travel

---

a: (a) Acts 2:14-36.

along with thousands of other areas of design such as bio-chemical, medicine, micro-chip technology, and atomic. Keep in mind that it is God who has given mankind this ability to design and then produce.

God's Design of a Close Freewill Loving Righteous Family

Now, let's consider one of God's designs that is far more complex. Let's consider designing a freewill loving intimate righteous family made up of individuals living within a complex material-spiritual universe. The eternal mature intimate mutually-interactive family is the most complex part of this Creation. Let's consider the variables involved in giving each individual tremendous free will and keeping track and interacting with each individual from the beginning of the Creation to the end all prior to implementing the physical Creation. God's ongoing interaction with all was planned out prior to implementing the physical Creation to help each become the best that they would be capable and willing to become. Our amazing Heavenly Father working with His Son and Holy Spirit was not limited by time and knew exactly what He was going to do to help each individual become the best that they were willing to become for eternity.[a]

As the Father and Son worked out the details of the Creation prior to implementing it,[8] They also worked out a plan to send the Son into Their Creation at just the right time to teach people truth[b] and die a death that would eternally remove bad actions from all people of all time who learned to return Their love and follow Their leadership.[c] This would make it possible for those who returned Their love to become part of Their eternal sinless family to live with Them within the New Heaven and New Earth separate from all those who chose to live self-centered

---

a: (a) predestination based on foreknowledge: Eph 1:4-6; 1 Peter 1:1-2;
(b) what was real and what was false: John 18:37; (c) John 3:14-17;
1 Peter 2:9, 24; 2 Cor 5:21.

lives.[a] Consider the many variables within such a design and creation where the Creator is working with each individual to move as many as will listen toward social interaction that maintains care and equality for all.

How much deviation from perfect righteousness should be allowed as part of the process for each freewill individual in such a creation? The more free will allowed, the greater the variations away from pure righteousness, but in the long run, the greater free will allows for more mature equalitarian loving interactive relationships within the family of God. It is understandable that if all free will was removed there would be no variations in righteousness, and therefore, God's robotic family would not need any help in learning the difference between good and evil. But, because of God's desire for a mature freewill intimate sinless *mutually-interactive* family, His design includes a way of removing all wrong behavior from everyone within the Creation who receives Him and His way of life. The Father, Son, and Holy Spirit worked out this very complex design; and after a six day start-up and seeing that all was moving toward Their desired outcome, God stated that the Creation was "good exceedingly [Gen 1:31]."

As we reflect further on God's Creation and His ability to produce a perfected Creation, we notice at least four key points: (1) the Father, Son, and Holy Spirit (the tri-unity of God) initially created man in Their own image according to Their own likeness ("Their=Our": Gen 1:26-27) in a sinless *physical* state;[b] (2) God gave humanity a fairly large amount of free will in order to create a close *mature mutually-interactive* relationship with as many as would come to desire the same; (3) God knew prior to the initial physical start of the Creation that all humanity would be cloaked in sin through Adam and Eve's initial sin; and therefore, all of the Creation would enter a corrupted state;[c] and (4) God knew that He alone had the ability to restore those who learned to return His love to a sinless state that would be higher than Adam and Eve's original state, a *resurrected spiritual-physical* state. This higher state shares qualities both of flesh and spirit realms simultaneously,

---

a: (a) Rev 21:7-8; (b) Gen 2:7; (c) Rev 13:8; Rom 8:18-22.

which matches Jesus' final state.[a] Keep in mind that this same Jesus is the Incarnate Word (*logos*) of the Father who created the whole material universe under His Father's direction.[b]

Desiring an interactive give-and-take loving relationship within His eternal holy family, God's final outcome of the Creation allows His holy family to live with Him forever in a very close mutually-interactive mature relationship with no more pain and chaos.[c] Those who reject God's love and/or lordship have to wait in a holding place similar to our modern jails waiting for the Great White Throne Judgment.[d] This holding place (jail) is called Sheol in the Old Testament and Hades in the New Testament.[e] When compared, Ps 16:10 and Acts 2:27 show the equality of the terms "Sheol" and "Hades." At the Great White Throne Judgment, all in lower Sheol/Hades will eventually stand trial before Jesus and be condemned to live an eternally isolated life away from God, His holy Family, and other righteous heavenly beings in a place called the "Lake of Fire," "Hell," or "Gehenna."

With God's highly freewill Creation, some still question whether or not God has given His Creation enough free will to make such an important decision as whether or not to return His love and welcome His lordship in order to receive spiritual birth (salvation). Scripture is clear that each person is ultimately responsible for this eternal life decision and that God patiently works with *all* to turn each from self-centeredness to Him and His way of caring life, which is sometimes called "repentance."[x][f]

Knowing that God *is able* to bring everyone of all time into His holy family, it is clear that if salvation were solely up to God, without each individual choosing whether or not that they would receive Him into their lives, *all would be saved*! In reality, just as God instructed Israel to learn to love Him back, stay close to Him (trust Him), and obey His commandments in order to live a blessed

---

a: (a) Phil 3:20-21; (b) Heb 1:1-2; John 1:1-3; 4:34; 7:16-17; 8:28-29, 47; Col 1:13-20; (c) Rev 21:1-4; 2 Peter 3:10-11; cf. Dan 12:1-2; Matt 25:34, 46; (d) Rev 20:11-15; (e) 1 Sam 2:6; 2 Sam 22:6; Ps 16:8-11; 88:3; 89:48; Ezek 26:20; Luke 16:19-31; Acts 2:25-28; Rev 20:13; (f) 2 Peter 3:9; John 3:16; Eph 1:13-14.

life in the Promised Land, everyone within the Creation must make a similar decision in order to live a blessed life now and an eternal sinless life with God after physical death.[a]

Everyone has an equal opportunity to listen to God[b] and must decide whether or not to do so. While Abraham was living in upper Sheol, he told a rich man who had died and ended up in lower Sheol that even if an individual came back from the dead to speak with people about life, it would not make any difference if they did not listen to Moses (first five books of the Bible) and the prophets.[c] God wants people to learn to be socially responsible for one another as the Holy Spirit helps them understand God and His Creation. Looking forward to the time when the Creation will come to its completion and living conditions will have been peaceful under Jesus' rule for generations, we learn that for a short time, Satan will be set free to temp humanity again, and under his leadership, a great number of people will join him to go against God.[d] No matter what the living conditions are, good or bad, many will not learn to return God's love, follow His righteous way of life, not submit to His leadership.

Secondly, some might question God's level of love for all. If God truly loves everyone so much, why would He allow those who do not want to be part of His eternal holy family to actually live in an isolated place like Hell knowing that they will suffer unrest and pain forever? Some think that it would be more loving of God to end their lives. Consider this: would it be fair to give someone an ample amount of free will only to kill them if they do not chose to follow your loving way of life? From the Bible, it is clear that God values life greatly, and therefore, all who become a life will live forever no matter what choices they make, but it is also clear that those who reject God and His way of life will have eternal consequences that are appropriate for their actions.[e]

Let's keep in mind that God cares about all, including those who reject Him, and therefore encourages everyone throughout their lives to do what is loving and righteous even if He knows that

---

a: (a) Deut 30:15-20; Rom 6:22; 8:28-30; (b) Rom 2:11-16; (c) Luke 16:29-31; (d) Rev 20:7-10; (e) Rev 20:13.

they will end up rejecting Him and His leadership. Also, keep in mind that God knew prior to the physical implementation of His Creation who would learn to return His love and follow His lead and who would not; there are no surprises for God.

The Creation Is Moving toward Its Final Form

This is God's creation! He knows what He is doing, and He is totally capable of completing it perfectly! After the start of His Creation, God considered what He had done and where it was headed according to His plans, and He said that it was "good exceedingly [Gen 1:31]." Prior to physically starting the Creation, God knew how each of us from the beginning to the end would respond to His love and lordship (foreknowledge).[a] When we consider God's end goal, His perfected family living in the New Heaven and New Earth, we realize that His creation is not over until He has separated His completed volunteer family from all who would not learn to love, trust, and obey Him from all generations and nations.

So, how active is God during the creation process? With so much evil going on due to ample free will, some question God's day-to-day involvement in His own Creation. Let's consider the fact that even though God asks all humanity to take care of one another and life in general,[b] it is God–not us–who has been doing the heavy lifting throughout the entire creative process. Although God is sovereign, He is also a serving sustainer[c] asking us to learn to do likewise.[d] Keep in mind that the Sent Son of God, Jesus, was born in a manger but could have been born in a palace if the Father so desired, and that He grew up doing manual labor as a carpenter's son instead of growing up as an earthly prince or king.

Not being limited by time, God knew in advance what it would take to create a mature freewill intimate loving righteous (holy) family. He knew ahead of time throughout the whole

---

a: (a) Eph 1:3-8; 1 Peter 1:1-2; Rom 8:28-30; (b) Gen 1:26-28;
(c) Matt 20:28; Mark 10:45; Luke 22:27; (d) John 13:5-17.

Creation who would want to become part of His eternal loving family and therefore receive Him as lord as well as savior. These are the "called" and "chosen" of God.[a] The Father also knew in advance that it was necessary (*dei*) to send His Son, Jesus, to die for all humanity[b] in order to bring those who would learn to love Him into a final eternal sinless resurrected state.

So, prior to starting the physical Creation, the Father, Son, and Holy Spirit planned out a death within the Trinity (Tri-unity). They would suffer tremendously as the Son died a physical death and was also separated from the Father (spiritual death) taking on the bad actions of all people over the entire Creation[c] of those who learned to trust Them. For those who would learn to trust and obey Them out of a developing love for all, Jesus would remove their sin taking each's bad actions onto Himself[d] in order to eliminate it forever after spending His three days in Sheol/Hades. These three days might have seemed a lot longer to Him as He was separated from His Heavenly Father due to our sins.[e] After His atoning death and three days in Sheol/Hades,[f] the resurrected Jesus again became the "righteous" one.[g] Although we cannot remove bad actions (sin) from one another, if we could, it might be comparable to someone being able to remove all cancerous cells from someone else by personally absorbing these bad cells into himself and replacing them with his own healthy cells and in the end dying due to the cancer now ravaging his own body.

God makes sure that no matter what circumstance one is born into, everyone will understand that He desires **all** to be part of His family and live holy lives.[h] Although everyone is born into sin under the many deceptions of Satan, all have a chance to overcome evil as God teaches **everyone** the reality of His Creation and His requirements for eternal life,[i] which eventually brings some to the point of wanting to do His will and follow His holy ways.[j]

---

a: (a) Matt 25:34; Rom 8:28; Eph 1:3-5; 1 Peter 1:1-5; (b) John 3:14-15; (c) Heb 10:10-14; (d) Gal 3:13-14; 1 Peter 2:24; 2 Cor 5:21; Col 2:13-14; Rev 21:3-4; (e) 2 Peter 3:8; (f) Matt 12:39-40; (g) 1 John 2:1, 29; 3:3-5; cf. Heb 1:1-3; (h) 2 Peter 3:9; 1 Tim 2:4; cf. Rev 3:20; (i) Rom 2:11-16; in this light, consider Rom 1:18-32; (j) Matt 12:50; 1 John 2:17.

God Wants To Be Your Friend

In the perfected eternal world that God is creating, there has to be pure righteous leadership in order to keep the family cohesively living together without sin. Therefore, during our physical life, *individuals must decide if God is worthy of their love, respect, and obedience*. In this process, God takes the lead and helps everyone know Him and His righteous way of life asking everyone to learn to love, trust, and obey Him.[a] Jesus is the perfect example of the loving, trusting, and obedient Son doing those things that please His Heavenly Father at all times.[b] In addition, Jesus told His present and future obedient disciples that not only were they family members,[c] but that they were also His friends and that there is no greater love than someone being willing to die for his friends.[d] Within God's family, all members are friends with one another. When Peter was challenged by Jesus to help guide the Church, He asked Peter three times if he really loved Him. Peter responded each time telling Jesus that he loved Him as a good friend, which is the closest kind of relational love (John 21:15-17; *phileō* versus *agapaō*).

Getting Off the Wide-Road That Leads to Destruction

Knowing that God wants everyone to learn to return His love,[e] why do so many stay on the wide-road (life-path) that leads to a lower quality life now and an eventual permanent separation from God instead of receiving God into their lives?[f] With God doing so much to help everyone have a better life, it would seem that most people would get off the wide-road leading to destruction and follow God's path for their lives. But in reality, an elevated sense of self-worth (pride) along with Satan's encouragement to

---

a: (a) John 14:15, 21, 23; 15:10; (b) John 4:34; 8:28-29; and others; (c) John 20:14; cf. 17:20-23; (d) John 15:13-14; (e) John 3:16; 2 Peter 3:9; (f) Matt 7:13-14.

rebel continually against God keeps many content to follow their own desires instead of God's. With the many distractions of general life, if we ignore God speaking to our hearts (God's self-revelation), we will fail to know and love Him for who He is. He is a loving caring creator and father. Our primary obligation is to learn to love God back. He is constantly working with us and worthy of our love.[a] Secondly, if we want to be with God, we must allow Him to break through our personal activity and Satan's deceptions and teach us to start to love others in addition to loving ourselves and our families.[b]

It was not long after the start of the Creation that Satan called God a liar regarding death (separation from God) through disobedience and tempted Eve and Adam to sin against God resulting in their immediate separation from Him (spiritual death).[c] This was the start of our present fallen world. Everyone starts with a corrupted nature due to Adam and Eve's initial sin and the additional sins committed over hundreds and hundreds of years by those who have gone before us. Then, we add the consequences of our personal sins to the mix. This corruption is shared by all on some level, and, therefore, sin affects all. But, as we look at the world and our fallen nature and compare it to the purity of our loving Creator, some of us have come to a point in our lives that we want a change for the better. We want a pure godly life and, therefore, we have called out for a savior.[d]

What complicates matters further is not only the fact that all are born into sin, but, in reality, we are all born into an ongoing war initiated by Satan against God.[e] God could have locked Satan up at any time even prior to or during the Creation, and eventually, He will do just that.[f] But, it is clear that God allows Satan to remain present to tempt us to rebel against Him in order to force us to think about our own fallen nature, His goodness, and the future sinless New Heaven and New Earth.[g]

We should also keep in mind that God's Anointed Messiah, Jesus, did not come to bring peace to the whole world but instead

---

a: (a) Deut 30:19-20; Matt 22:36-37; 1 John 4:16; (b) Matt 22:39; John 13:34; (c) Gen 3:1-6, 24; (d) Isa 6:1-8; Acts 4:12; Gal 3:24; (e) Matt 11:12; 1 Peter 5:8-11; Rev 12:7-11; (f) Rev 20:10; (g) Rev 21.

to divide it between those who are willing to follow God and His righteous ways and those who are not.[a] Although we do not presently have world peace, let's thank God that Jesus came to bring eternal peace to all who learn to listen to Them.[b]

God has a continuous open door policy for all who voluntarily submit to His lordship forgiving and removing our sin and reconciling us into His eternal family through a second birth, a spiritual birth. So, as we continue to reflect on God and His goodness, we come to realize that He expects us to listen to Him because He is our Creator and Father, who loves us beyond measure and constantly works on our behalf. Everything that He wants to teach us is for our personal and collective good. God teaches us that true joy and inner peace come from dying to our self-centered aspirations and joining Him in serving one another.[c]

Being part of God's eternal intimate loving righteous family brings about joy and inner peace that cannot be duplicated by any perversion of God's lifestyle meant for all. Jesus wants our joy to be full, which can only be accomplished by following Him.[d] As we follow God's leadership and allow Him to transform us, the Holy Spirit helps us to be more and more like Jesus, which helps us grow in love, joy, peace, patience, kindness, goodness, faithfulness, gentleness, and self-control.[e]

---

a: (a) Matt 10:34-39; Luke 12:49-53; (b) Eph 2:14-16; cf. John 16:33; (c) Luke 9:23; 14:26-27, 33; and others; (d) John 15:11; 17:13; Heb 12:1-2; cf. Col 1:24; (e) Gal 5:22-23; cf. 1 Cor 13.

2

—

Experiencing Good & Evil Demands a Decision

Even if you not yet come to a place of trusting God, it is highly probable that you have sensed an ongoing battle of evil trying to prevail over good. Most of us have come to realize that there is a way of life that is beneficial and many ways of life that ultimately bring harm to ourselves and others. The way that we live with others makes a real difference in the here-and-now and in the future. In reality, God has created the universe with real absolute standards for all life. When we follow His rules, we do good for ourselves and others, when we do not, we harm ourselves and others, which is bad, evil. Because God is communicating to all, on some level, everyone is aware of God and His standards.[a]

Not only are most aware of the difference between evil and good, all participate in doing both. There is plenty of wrongdoing by all. No one is completely innocent. Everyone has fallen short of living out a perfectly righteous life according to God's standards *except Jesus Christ.*[b] Evil is recognized by most societies around the world, and due to the harm done through evil actions, more time is spent keeping current on the latest evil than on good. Whether ignoring someone, speaking an unkind word, not helping someone whom God puts in our path, directly disobeying God's instructions for our lives, lying, cheating, stealing, killing, enslaving, sexually abusing, or doing some other form of evil, we all see and do some evil.

---

a: (a) Rom 1:18-32; 2:11-16; (b) Rom 3:23; Isa 53:4-9; 2 Cor 5:21; 1 Peter 2:21-24.

Evil versus Good

Personally, we have all experienced times in our lives in which we have done something that has hurt someone else and have either felt immediate or eventual remorse. Even if someone has not been walking in spiritual awareness of God's presence and continual teaching, most recognize the fact that we all struggle with self-centered desires. Whether we listen to the leading of God or not, He talks to all and moves as many as listen into a place of awareness that helps make good choices easier.[a]

We all need to listen to God more carefully, because He will help us look past our self-centered desires and block Satan's deceptions and noise.[b] Satan's deceptions and noise are generated by many sources to include entertainment, technological gadgets, and even so-called friends at times. If we do not listen to God, we are controlled in some way by Satan, the Evil One.[c] God desires to develop our individual consciences and teach each of us our assigned good works.[d] If we ignore or do not hear God's voice, it is easy to miss out on what is really going on including the blessings that come from living out our lives within God's will.

Even with those who are hostile toward God and His followers,[e] God stays at work in everyone's life bringing as many as possible to a place of turning from self-centered lifestyles to Him and His righteous way of life.[f] This is biblically called *repentance*. God wants everyone to come to a place in his or her life that allows Him to teach them about His genuine concern and love for all, which in turn encourages many to come to Him for everyday help and eternal salvation.[g]

Although many listen to God enough to know the difference between good and evil, there are many who have not listened well enough to know that *our world is caught up in the middle of two powerful kingdoms at war:* the Kingdom of God

---

a: (a) John 8:31b-32; 16:8-11; (b) 2 Cor 4:3-4; (c) 1 John 5:19; (d) Phil 2:13; Eph 2:10; 1 Cor 12:18; (e) Rom 5:10; John 17:14-15; (f) Lev 19:1-2; 2 Peter 3:9; cf. Rom 1:18-32; 2:11-16; (g) 1 John 4:16; cf. Gal 3:26-29.

and the Kingdom of Hell presently ruled by Satan. God and His kingdom are more powerful and at the appropriate time will put Satan and his followers in an isolated place forever called Hell, the Lake of Fire, or Gehenna. But, until that happens, God has been using Satan to force everyone to evaluate the good and evil around them and decide on which lifestyle they desire for eternity. Because all of us live out our lives doing and experiencing both good and evil, *each has to decide* if they want a close relationship with God and those who are listening to Him, or do they prefer to reject God's lordship and way of life knowing that this alternative gives some freedom from His leadership but leads to a downward spiral toward eventual eternal shame, unrest, and suffering.

Satan is out to deceive as many as possible trying to keep them from listening to God so that they will never really get to know Him or His Word. God on the other hand, wants everyone to understand reality and consider carefully their future. When individuals start listening to God because of His great love and concern for all, He starts to mold and shape them into His own image. On the other hand, for those who do not listen, God allows Satan to continue to deceive them into thinking that they are going to have an abundant joyful life *on their own terms*. Whatever one ultimately decides determines one's *eternal destiny*. No matter where you stand, you should stay alert knowing that our world is actually in the middle of a major spiritual war with *eternal consequences* and that God will eventually separate those who want to be with Him and His way of life from those who do not. God rescues (*malat*) those who listen to Him from the long-term consequences of bad actions.[a]

If you could look ahead in time and get a glimpse of both future kingdoms in their final states and see God and His perfected family living in love, peace, and joy, and Satan and those who follow in his footsteps continually hurting one another, what would you be willing to do for yourself and others in order to live with God and His family forever? In reality, God has already made a way for you to do this through Jesus Christ.[b] *If you really would*

---

a: (a) Dan 12:2; cf. Matt 25:45-46; Rom 2:11-13; Gal 6:7; Rev 20:12;
(b) Rom 1:16-17.

like to know God better in order to follow Him, God will help you live out a more fulfilling life in the here-and-now experiencing His love, peace, and joy as part of your growing relationship with Him and the Church.[(a)]

Spiritual Warfare in General

From now on, *be continually strengthened in the Lord in the strength of His might.* Put on all of the armor of God in order to enable yourselves to stand before the scheming of the Devil, *because our battle is not against blood and flesh*, but instead against the leaders, the authorities, the cosmic powers of this darkness, the spirits of evil in the heavenly places.   Eph 6:10-12[9]

Let's keep in mind that the Creation is God's work! As He enlarges His intimate close-knit holy family, Satan continually keeps fighting hard against Him and His growing family. There came a time in his fight against God that Satan encouraged Israel's religious leaders to crucify Jesus, but to his surprise *instead of getting rid of the Father's only Son, he unknowingly lost the battle to separate all of God's children from their Creator for eternity, and instead of no sons, there will be many sons*.

God teaches us through John 3:14-16 that Jesus' death on humanity's behalf *was necessary* in order to remove sin for all those who were trusting God for help in their present condition and redemption of their souls for eternity. As we consider the entire Creation, God teaches us in Hebrews 10:4-10 that Jesus' death removes sin not only for those who were trusting God in Jesus' day, but for all who learned to love, trust, and obey God from the beginning of the Creation until its finalization after Christ's thousand-year reign and the last battle with Satan.[(b)]

From the time of Jesus' death on the Cross and Satan's realization that he had lost the battle for the souls of all humanity,

---

a: (a) Rom 6:22-23; (b) Rev 20:7-10.

he has been doing his best *to minimize God's victory.*[a] Satan has been doing his best to distract, placate, intimidate, and mislead as many people as possible so that they will not take the time to figure out what eternity will be like without God's presence.[b] Over the centuries, as God has been building His eternal family and filling His eternal Kingdom with loving righteous individuals, Satan has come to realize that his time is becoming short. Because of this, Satan has been escalating his attacks in the last couple hundred years. Satan is striving to silence God's obedient children on earth, as he continues to deceive those who are not following God.[c]

This Is Personal

If you are a committed follower of Jesus, have you ever wondered why some of the good things that you wish to do seem so difficult to start and accomplish although part of you knows that it should be easier? Does it seem that during the times when you want to do some good knowing that God has put something special in your heart, you seem to be swimming in molasses instead of water? If this is the case, you have experienced spiritual warfare firsthand. You may have come to realize that many of your own doubts and hesitations coupled with circumstances around you were *not* just part of the natural order of everyday life. In many cases, they were caused by acts of spiritual warfare against you and the godly actions that you were contemplating.[d]

Satan and his followers are constantly trying to influence Christ's followers looking for ways to hinder or stop completely what God has laid on their hearts.[e] As God's children pray and seek God's will for their individual and collective lives, they need to be aware–as Daniel was–that this ongoing battle is ultimately God's. Although no human can see the spiritual realm, God has included His good angels in the battles to work with His obedient children. God's angels are helping Jesus' followers on an ongoing basis.[f] Those who follow Jesus are used by God to help awaken

---

a: (a) 1 Cor 15:55-57; (b) Rev 12:9, 12; (c) 1 John 3:7-13; cf. 5:18-19; Rev 3:16; (d) Eph 6:12; (e) Eph 2:10; (f) Heb 1:13-14.

and rescue those who are not paying attention as the spiritual battles rage between the kingdoms of Good and Evil until the end of this Messianic Age.

This Is Ongoing

During the reigns of Darius, King of Chaldea, and Cyrus, King of Persia, God gave Daniel visions showing him future events.[a] We see from Daniel's vision during the third year of Cyrus, that there was ongoing spiritual warfare just as today. One of Satan's angels, who was in a leadership position over Persia, had slowed one of God's angels down for 21 days until God's lead angel, Michael, came to his aid. Michael's intervention allowed God's assigned angel to go to Daniel and give him insight regarding His plans in all that was transpiring.[b] This messenger from God stated that as soon as he had given Daniel God's vision, he was going right back to continue his fight against the same demonic leader in Persia as well as engage in a battle against one of Satan's angels who was heading up warfare in Greece.[c] Even today, Satan consistently wages war with those who faithfully follow God.

Approximately five hundred years later, we learn that the same type of ongoing spiritual warfare was continuing. Paul stated that Satan had slowed him down when wanting to visit and encourage the Thessalonians whom he had led to the true Messiah.[d] Satan is consistently waging war against God's obedient children causing as much stumbling, suffering, and damage as possible;[e] but if we listen to God, He will use our trials and tribulations to help others and build our character.[f]

Daniel's account and Paul's warning about the bad angels who are helping Satan should be a wake-up call for all of us. This is not a game with simple consequences. This ongoing war between good and evil has eternal consequences for all. In Daniel's

---

a: (a) Dan 9-10; (b) Dan 10:12-14; (c) Dan 10:20; (d) 1 Thess 2:18; (e) e.g. 1 Thess 2:14-16; 3:4; 2 Thess 1:4-5; cf. Luke 16:13; (f) Rom 5:3-5.

account above, God could have helped his angels overcome Satan faster or even immediately, but He works in such a way that His angels become more skilled through experience just as He works with Jesus' followers.[a] Jesus' followers are required to do some things partially in their own strength in order for God to develop their character,[b] but they should always remember that ultimately, it is in Christ's strength that we overcome evil forces.[c]

Jesus did not ask our Heavenly Father to remove any of His followers from the evil of this world, but He did ask the Father to protect His followers from the Evil One through His name. Jesus' followers are part of His family and will be protected accordingly by God as part of His holy family.[d] Whenever Jesus' followers fall short in any given battle or circumstance, God helps them do their part whether they physically live or die.[e] The ultimate goal is helping as many as possible know God well to trust Him.

Spiritual Warfare & Satan's Deceptions

Do not be amazed, for *Satan transforms (disguises) himself as an angel of light*. Therefore, it is not a great thing if indeed his servants transform/disguise themselves as servants of righteousness whose end shall be according to their works.   2 Cor 11:14-15

There is a common thread to all of Satan's scheming and attacks on humanity. Satan wants to take over God's Creation and His authority. He has turned a third of the angels in Heaven against God[f] and now wishes to keep as many of us as possible from listening to God. The truth of the matter is that whoever is not listening to God, is in reality fighting against God whether knowingly or not.[g] Jesus said, "By their finished works you will know them [Matt 7:16a]."

---

a: (a) 2 Thess 3:1; Heb 1:14; 5:14; (b) Rom 5:3-5; Heb 12:1-3; cf. 2:10; (c) Eph 6:10; (d) John 17:11, 15-17; (e) 1 John 2:25-27; 4:4; (f) Rev 12:4; (g) John 8:42-47; Eph 2:1-3; 1 John 5:19.

If Satan can keep people concentrating on themselves and their families, in reality, he has kept them from knowing God and His love for all. If people start listening to God, some will start obediently interacting with Him, and God will develop within them a loving trust for Him due to His love and faithfulness. Those who choose to listen to God and obey Him will eventually come to a place in their lives of repentance and spiritual birth into His eternal holy family.

The Wide-road Leading to Destruction

In his battle for ultimate control over everything, Satan has been constantly trying to preoccupy humanity with itself, scare humanity into submission, and/or turn humanity from God through the introduction of many counterfeit gods and religious structures. Some of these counterfeits scare people into submission and others enable people to remain self-centered living for themselves and their families.

Satan has filled our world with counterfeits to replace God. Because Satan has not been able to remove knowledge of our Creator from humanity, he has created a myriad of religious institutions to confuse many. In reality, through deceptions and half truths, these false gods and hurtful philosophies satisfy many and help keep them away from the one true Creator. The last thing that Satan wants is for people to know reality.[a] In addition to riches, personal aspirations, entertainment, and even laziness, Satan uses individuals and fabricated religions such as Hinduism, Siddhartha Gautama (Buddhism), Mohammed (Moslems), Joseph Smith (Mormons), Charles Russell (Jehovah's Witnesses), and others to distort reality in order to make it harder for people to know their true creator. Even with all of Satan's cunning deceptions, he cannot completely disguise his deceptive false teachings because they *all* exhibit some of his personal attributes, some much more than others. The better that you come to know God and His Word, the easier it is to recognize Satan and his counterfeits.

----

a: (a) 2 Cor 4:3-4; cf. John 8:44.

Self-centeredness

If Satan can keep people thinking about themselves as the center of life, he has won. Due to the sin of God's first created, Adam and Eve, all are born into a self-centered, selfish world that is in constant rebellion against God and His standards.[a] Satan uses the desires of fallen humanity against itself. If an individual is focused primarily on himself or herself, Satan is quick to remove anything that these individuals may have heard that is true about God from the forefront of their thoughts and replace them with substitutes.[b]

Loss of the Familiar

As the Holy Spirit leads and individuals start thinking about God, Satan will try hard to make their lives miserable through many circumstances including the loss of friends and outbursts of others in the world. Satan knows that most people like what is familiar and will not move easily into unfamiliar realms to include friendships without a good reason.[c] But for those who step out even with a little faith, God is faithful to continue to draw them to Himself. He will teach them a better way of life based on a genuine concern for all.

Worldly Success

When one considers following Jesus, he or she may encounter an even greater hurdle than making new friends. Christ will start to reshape their priorities including redefining success, which may move Satan to tempt them with additional income. If he is able to keep them distracted with additional resources that require additional time, many will lose their developing spiritual connection to God and go back to following other gods including money.[d]

---

a: (a) Rom 5:6-10; (b) Matt 13:19; (c) Matt 13:20-21; (d) Matt 13:22.

Satan will do anything including offering additional monetary success to some in order to keep them from making a real commitment to God. It is amazing how good self-fulfillment through the elevation of self looks until one learns from God how much better His way of life is. But, if individuals who get this far in their walk with Jesus make a commitment *to deny themselves* and join God in building His eternal intimate holy family, God will continue to shape and mold them eventually bringing them closer and closer to Jesus' perfect moral image as they lead others to God out of a growing love for God and their fellow man.

Following Jesus and Intensifying Battles

For those who start following Jesus wanting to live their lives according to the Fathers' will and ways, the battles normally intensify. Satan has already lost the battle for their souls, so he now must concentrate on how many more souls will be pulled from his grasp through the individuals who have made a solid commitment to follow God's leading. Jesus' followers know that they are the light of the world and that God works through them, not around them. They are the hands and feet of God's Son who created everything physically.[a] If Satan can reduce Christian witness to the world by distracting them, he knows that he still has more opportunity to keep non-Christians in the dark and away from God.

In my own life, I have had many times when I became aware of God's desire for me to do some task that would help others both physically and spiritually. It seems that without fail all types of situations would come up to distract me from doing my assignment.[b] As I look back over more than forty years of following Christ as an adult with a genuine commitment, I pray that I have at least completed God's desired purposes fifty percent of the time. If we do not stay focused on Jesus,[c] it is easy to be sidetracked. I can recount everything from simple emergency repairs on our house or cars, to immediate family needs, to some other ministry needs, or even to expansion of current ministry or

---

a: (a) Eph 4:4; 1 Cor 12:13; (b) Matt 6:25-33; (c) Heb 12:1-3.

work that would try to pull me away from doing the current mission that God had asked me to complete. I know that I am not alone in experiencing this type of spiritual attack.

Success: a Continual Temptation

For some, even after committing to follow Jesus, Satan will continue to use a common distraction that transcends time. He will tempt Jesus' followers with additional revenue for their families, if they will just give up more of their time from serving God. Over the years, I have seen Satan use additional income to move many of my friends and acquaintances away from ministries that God had laid on their hearts. Many had become excited about what God had asked them to do, but before they became invested in God's work, they were faced with opportunities to make additional money for themselves and their families with additional work attached to that money. In many cases, they chose to forego God's ministry in order to obtain additional monetary security or simply to spend more on their own desires. Satan wins when we choose additional money over accepting God's assignments. We must all be diligent to listen to God, and then do what it takes to accomplish His will. I know from experience that God will see us through the spiritual and resulting physical and mental battles into success, if we faithfully do His will.

No Pain, No Gain

Another common deception permeating many of our churches today is the idea that God does not want us to work through anything that is difficult. Many of Christ's followers are led to believe that if something is difficult, God must be shutting the door to that assignment. Some of Jesus' followers just do not know any better, but there is a second group within our churches who do not know Jesus and therefore have no clue about what it means to deny themselves, pick up their individual crosses, and follow Him.[a] This group of potential followers of Jesus confuse those who are truly trying to follow Him, because Satan uses them to make complacency and other abnormalities look normal.[b]

The norm for a true Christian is *to be radically different* than the World as he or she tries to understand the leading of the Holy Spirit. All we have to do is look at the New Testament accounts of our forefathers as they ministered in the first century and realize that most went through many trials and tribulations as they followed Jesus. *Following Jesus is not suppose to be easy, but it should be fulfilling!* Following Jesus will not be easy because the battle over the outcome of every single life *is* significant. God loves everyone and wants all to come to a place in their lives where they will turn from their self-centered ways to Him and His ways, and in so doing be saved.[c] There are eternal consequences for our actions. Although at times it is difficult to follow Jesus, the outcome of faithful discipleship produces godly character, excitement, inner peace, and great joy.[d]

Meaningful Relationships

If Satan cannot sidetrack Jesus' followers from doing their God-given assignments through some form of additional work or adversity, he may try to keep them preoccupied from God's work through entertainment and/or entanglement in sins.[e] In America, I believe that the most benign type of diversion from God's will is entertainment. *If we are not careful, we will spend too much time* watching television, going to live performances, interacting in sports or other recreational activities, or just staying busy on our phones, computers, i-pads, and other gadgets without developing godly relationships.[10] *This is a sin!*

Satan has caused many to replace meaningful periods of work and social interaction with self-centered entertainment and/or technological activity that helps one feel productive but, in reality, only keeps one preoccupied. Many are now spending unnecessary

---

a: (a) Luke 14:26-27; (b) 2 Cor 11:14-15; (c) 2 Peter 3:9; (d) Rom 5:1-5; Gal 5:22; John 14:27; 15:8-11; 17:13; (e) Heb 12:1.

long periods each day texting, emailing, internet browsing, gaming, and all sorts of self-absorbing activities that are contrary to building solid godly relationships. This is one of the new opiums of the twenty-first century. *Self-centered activity and entertainment are easy. Working hard and building meaningful godly relationships takes time and effort but is rewarding.*

As we come to know God and His desire for our lives,[a] we begin to understand the importance of a close mature loving righteous (holy) relationship with God and one another. Even within everyday routines, Satan is at work destroying godly relationships through many perversions of things that God created for good.[b]

Consider food. God has created food to sustain our temporary physical bodies. Satan has caused many to substitute overeating, for godly intimate relationships. Overeating is easy; however building caring intimate relationships takes work.

Consider drugs. God has given us the wisdom to use certain chemicals to assist the body. Satan has caused many to misuse all types of drugs as a substitute for godly caring relationships that serve one another. The misuse of drugs is easy; however building caring relationships takes work.

Consider sex. God has created sex as one of our bodily functions in order to procreate building family units and potentially expanding His eternal holy family. It should also increase intimacy between a man and a woman within a life-long marriage relationship. Satan has caused many to substitute perverted forms of sex instead of building godly intimate caring relationships. Perverted sex is easy, but building a godly caring relationship between a man and a woman takes work. A godly single heterosexual relationship is the basis of a sound family structure for the proper edification of our children and in reality the whole human race. A godly home is extremely helpful in learning to love God and man; but beware, Satan is out to kill and destroy as many caring relationships as possible.[c] *Listen to God!* He will help you build solid caring relationships as you help the lost and hurting.[d]

---

a: (a) Titus 2:14; (b) 2 Tim 2:22-26; (c) 1 Peter 5:8; (d) Rev 3:20; John 15:1-11.

Stay Focused!

Reverence God and keep His commandments.

Eccl 12:13b

The writer of Ecclesiastes was dismayed at the end of his life after working hard and doing much. In reality, his efforts did not amount to much when looked at from an eternal perspective. Even if we work really hard and smart and acquire much, when we die we leave all material things to others who will do whatever they wish with their newly acquired possessions. This cycle will continue until God finishes His Creation. John Ortberg has written a book titled *It All Goes Back in the Box*,[11] which portrays this concept well. John uses the idea of winning Monopoly at any cost to illustrate the futility of winning in this world at any cost and not taking into consideration that when the game is over (your physical life), all the pieces go back into the box. No one keeps the physical things that he or she acquires when physical death comes, but the good relationships that we developed are eternally important.

Solomon came to a point late in his physical life where he realized that what really matters is our response to God while we journey through this side of eternity. Do we learn to reverence God and consequently abide by His standards and help others to know Him, which has eternal value,[a] or do we live foolishly building our personal empires and end up separated from God and forfeit an eternal life of love, peace, and joy with Him and His eternal holy family? Satan has been tempting humanity from the beginning of the Creation to live foolishly and end up living an eternal life of shame, unrest, and pain.

In reality, it is true for every generation that *if one does not stay focused on God and follow His lead*, Satan will deceive that individual into working against God and His Kingdom.[b] It makes no difference whether one is a school teacher, nurse, doctor, social worker, minister, or someone else who helps people as part of his

---

a: (a) Eccl 12:13-14; John 8:31b-32; 17:3; (b) John 8:12; 8:43-44; 2 Peter 1:4; 1 John 2:16.

or her life work, if that individual is not living under Jesus' lordship, Satan will be misleading him or her.

Consider Jesus' conversation with some of the religious zealots of His day who thought that they were walking with God. Scripture is clear that even though one may appear to be doing God's work, unless he or she is actually listening to God and *doing His will*, that individual is not part of His eternal holy family.[a] Jesus told those individuals who were claiming to serve God in His day that although they were biological descendants of Abraham, in reality, they were following the devil, Satan, which made him their father.[b] Jesus wanted them to understand the consequences of following personal desires through Satan's deceptions, which were leading them away from God. Instead, they should have been listening carefully to God and following His way of life.

When you consider Jesus' ministry and all of the good that He did, how could so many supposedly godly people turn on Him and want Him crucified? Jesus' very fulfillment came from doing His Father's will,[c] yet Satan led many of Jesus' contemporaries to a place where they were blind to the identity of the Son of God. In the end, they even openly stated that they had no king other than Caesar.[d] What happened to God being their king? Satan is very good at deception and continues to deceive as many as possible including Jesus' followers today whenever they are not alert.

Today, many of our local churches are slumbering so soundly that they are ignoring their most important calling, which is to proclaim the goodness and purposes of God to those who do not know Him. Somehow, Satan has blinded many in our local churches about the joy of witnessing to the lost and the contemporary benefit to their families and the world when one walks in holiness, which culminates in the future benefit of walking in eternal perfection with God. Satan has somehow even deceived a fairly large number of regular church attendees to ignore some of God's teachings on righteous living (sanctification) and helping others to know God (witnessing). Nevertheless, Jesus made it clear that all of God's instructions for life are eternal.[e]

---

a: (a) Matt 7:21-23; John 7:17; (b) John 8:37-44, 47; (c) John 4:34; (d) John 19:15; (e) Matt 5:17-20; Luke 16:16-17.

Over the years, Satan has convinced many to believe lies that are worse than the one that he told Adam and Eve because their consequences are eternal. As in the beginning, Satan called God a liar.[a] Since then, one of his extremely dangerous lies teaches that God has lied to everyone in His Word, and in reality, no one will experience an eternal separation from Him called the Second Death, Hell.[b] Through this lie, he states that everyone goes to Heaven whether they listen to God or not because God loves them too much to allow anyone to go to Hell. In reality, it is because God loves everyone so much that He will not force anyone to join Him and His eternal close-knit holy family. In reality, everyone must personally choose to receive Him into their everyday lives and willingly submit to His leadership in order to enter into His eternal presence. It is through trust and obedience based on a growing love that one becomes an eternal holy family member, and only family members enter into Heaven.

And, for those who trust God and know from His Word that eternal separation from God is real, Satan has come up with another lie and is now trying to convince some that eternity is not really eternal. He is attempting to convince as many as possible that the Church has not understood God's Word correctly for the last 2000 years. Satan is now teaching that those who go to Hell will only go for a short time, but it will feel like being there for eternity. *What a surprise!* Satan is at it again. He continues to lie in order to bring about death for as many as possible, but God's Word is clear: individuals who reject Him and His way of life during this part of their eternal lives will be isolated from Him *forever* at the end of the Creation.

---

a: (a) Gen 3:1-5; John 8:44; (b) Rev 20:11-15.

3

Understanding the Basics of Spiritual Warfare

> From the days of John the Baptist until now, the
> Kingdom of the Heavens is suffering violence
> (*biazetai*), and violent ones are taking it by force.
>   Matt 11:12

> The Law and the prophets stood until John; from
> then the *Good News* of the Kingdom of God *is
> being proclaimed* (*euangelizetai*) and *everyone is
> forcing himself* (*biazetai*) into *it*. But, it is easier for
> the Heaven and Earth to pass away than for one
> stroke of a letter of the Law to fall/fail.
>   Luke 16:16-17

Everyone is trying to force their way into Heaven! Today,
Satan is still at war with those whom God created to be part of His
holy family blinding and deceiving as many as possible. All
humanity lives in a world caught up in war between two kingdoms,
God's and the rebels', whose main leader is Satan. Satan is a self-
proclaimed ruler who decided before the Creation to overthrow
God, steal what He owns, and rule it all.[a] After Christ's thousand-
year reign at the end of the Creation just for a brief moment, Satan
will be allowed to lead once again those who are not listening to
God.[b] After this final rebellion, Satan will be permanently isolated
from God and all righteous ones. He will be placed with other
rebellious souls in the eternal Lake of Fire, Hell.[c]

It is clear from Scripture that God's Creation is full of
bloody battles with evil trying to overcome good for eternity. John

---

a: (a) Matt 4:8-10; Eph 6:12; (b) John 12:31; 16:11; Rev 12:12;
(c) John 8:44; Matt 25:41; Rev 20:10.

the Baptist died proclaiming that the Messiah and His Kingdom had come. Jesus died representing God as He demonstrated the love of God through His actions and words. Most of Jesus' main disciples died proclaiming the truth about God's plan of salvation for those who would follow Jesus. Over the centuries, thousands upon thousands have died as they followed Jesus through the leading of the Holy Spirit.

Jesus said that He did not come into our world to produce world peace but instead division between those who would learn to follow Him and those who would not.[a] Jesus also said that although many were trying to force their way into the Kingdom of Heaven, it would not happen. God has the final say and His conditions–given through the Law and prophets–will stand. It was easier for the heavens and the earth to be totally destroyed than for God's Word to fail.[b] It is clear through His Word, the Bible, that God's plans shall be accomplished without fail!

As you study Scripture, you come to realize that our Heavenly Father has had everything under control from the very beginning. He sent Jesus into our world to teach us further revelation and then at just the right time, He died for all.[c] God teaches us that this battle between His Kingdom and the Kingdom of Hell will come to an end in God's perfect time when the Kingdom of Heaven is filled with God's new children.[d] God's Kingdom is commonly called the Kingdom of Heaven, and because of Jesus' redemptive work, it is also called the Kingdom of His Beloved Son, the Kingdom of Christ.[e]

When Jesus became incarnate and ministered among us, He brought God's Kingdom to us.[f] Jesus taught the world that those who walk according to God's eternal loving righteous ways are blessed now and forever.[g]

As we consider our participation in the battle going on around us, we all must eventually ***make a decision*** regarding our ***eternal allegiance***. On this large battlefield called earth, there has been and continues to be many deceivers teaching many false

---

a: (a) Luke 12:49-51; (b) Luke 16:16-17; cf. Isa 40:8; Matt 5:17-20;
(c) Gal 4:4; Acts 2:23; 4:27-28; (d) Matt 13:47-48; 22:1-14; (e) Col
1:13; Eph 5:5; (f) Matt 4:17; 12:28; (g) Matt 5:1-10; 7:21; 18:4.

concepts about the one true God, whose name is YHWH, and His holy nature. As we discussed earlier, there are many non-existent fabricated gods who stand in for Satan. They are presented to humanity as substitutes to replace YHWH. *Satan uses these shadows of himself* to distort reality and keep people from knowing their loving Creator and His desire for an eternal mature close loving-kind (holy) family. Additional information on Satan's created gods and religious institutions can be studied through books such as Josh McDowell's *A Ready Defense*.[12]

God's Anointed One, Jesus, the true prophesied Messiah, came to lead people into the light teaching reality and saving them from eternal separation from the one true Creator God. Jesus came bringing abundant life to all who listen here-and-now and for eternity.[a] Jesus is the only access to our Heavenly Father.[b] If Jesus' followers stay focused on Christ and follow Him, they will not be deceived so easily by Satan and will lead many into the light to meet God.[c] But, as the battle for the souls of humanity continues on through the creation process, we understand from God that there are many who will stay in the dark (keep things hidden) in order to do things for themselves at the expense of others and that God will not force them to change. They must change of their own free will.[d]

After the Cross

> After this, Jesus knowing that everything had now been completed in order to fulfill Scripture said, "I am thirsty." . . . Therefore, when He received the sour wine, Jesus said, *"It has been completed,"* and having bowed His head, He delivered up His spirit.
> John 19:28-30

Now, after the Cross, it is different. Those who obeyed God prior to the Cross along with all who are obeying God through

---

a: (a) John 10:10; (b) John 10:9; 14:6; Eph 2:18; (c) Matt 5:14-16; John 15:1-2; (d) Matt 7:13; John 1:9-13; 3:19-20; 2 Thess 2:10-12.

submission to Jesus' leadership after the Cross have a close eternal relationship with God. Through Jesus' death on the Cross, everyone who has ever lived in obedience to God will end up being made perfectly righteous living with God as part of His intimate holy family.[a] The greatest part of the pain of the childbirth of God's eternal holy family was over after the Cross.[b]

Satan knowing that his time was getting shorter and shorter began in a renewed intensity doing all that he could to hide the reality of Christ's victory over death (eternal separation from God).[c] Satan is still effectively deceiving many into thinking that everyone can choose whatever religion that suits them and still end up in the Kingdom of God. *Nothing could be further from the truth!* The Father has clearly spoken through His Son, Jesus of Nazareth, that Jesus is the only way (access) into His presence and kingdom.[d] No one will become a child of God through his or her own will, through the desire of family members and friends, nor through any other way except through Jesus.[e]

Resist Satan

When I consider a good friend and a former pastor of mine, Dr. Mark Corts, I remember a life that was anything but easy. God teaches us through the Apostle Peter to *resist Satan* and he will eventually flee.[f] Christ's followers should never flee spiritual battles because they serve the one true God, and He is able to overcome all enemies. God is able to overcome anything that Satan tries to do, and He is with and in all of His obedient children.[g]

Mark Corts was a follower of Christ who resisted Satan continuously doing what he knew to be right. He constantly had to deal with spiritual battles within his congregation, and for the last fifteen years of his life, he had to deal with ongoing spiritual battles intensified by physical illness. Mark wrote a book prior to his death entitled *The Truth about Spiritual Warfare: Your Place in the*

---

a: (a) Titus 2:14; Gal 3:13-14; Heb 10:4-10; (b) Ps 90:2; Rom 8:22; (c) John 17:4; 19:28-30; (d) John 14:6; (e) John 1:12-13; (f) 1 Peter 5:8-9; (g) John 14:23; 1 John 4:4.

Battle between God and Satan, which discusses some of his battles and spiritual warfare in general.[13] Because of his steadfast work in proclaiming God's Word and his resolve to do God's will at any cost, he became an effective contemporary role model. It was through Mark's willingness to give of himself and follow Jesus faithfully that I came to a place in my life at twenty eight where I was willing to do likewise and made a genuine commitment as an adult to follow Jesus to the best of my ability.

Under Mark's teaching, various Bible classes, and personal Bible study, Jesus not only became my active big brother looking out for me, but He also became *my lord* and *primary mentor.*[a] As I looked at Jesus' life on earth, I began to get a glimpse of what He had given up in Heaven[b] and suffered on earth in order to make a way for everyone's sins to be removed.[c] As I continued to study Scripture, the Apostle Paul became another mentor teaching me what faithful service looked like. When it was the right time, Jesus revealed Himself to Paul and corrected his understanding of God's plan of salvation.[d] From that point on, Paul was willing to give up his religious prestige and secure life in Judea and endure hardship after hardship[e] in order to proclaim the reality of the righteousness of God[f] and His atoning work through Christ.[g] Paul sacrificed everything in order to help rescue those who did not know God but were willing to listen to the Good News (Gospel) as he proclaimed it through his actions and words.[h]

Jesus did only good as He walked according to His Father's will, and He suffered greatly. Paul suffered greatly after he started following Jesus. Dr. Corts suffered much as he followed Jesus. In general, all who follow Jesus will be asked to give up some of what they could have had for themselves in this world, suffering loss in order to overcome the schemes of Satan.[i] Everything that God asks of His children helps others to see God's love and compassion for all, which in turn helps some come to their senses and ask Him for help in changing their lives to match His.[j]

---

a: (a) John 8:31-32; 1 John 2:27; (b) Phil 2:5-8; Heb 2:9-11; (c) 2 Cor 5:21; 1 Peter 2:24; (d) Acts 9:1-20; 22:1-16; Gal 1:11-17; (e) 2 Cor 11:22-31; Phil 2:4-12; (f) Rom 1:16-17; (g) John 3:16-17; (h) Phil 3:7-21; 2 Cor 11; (i) Luke 14:26-33; (j) Lev 19:1-2; 2 Cor 5:17-18.

Everything that God asks His obedient children to do will help others to see that there is a better way of life here-and-now and also for eternity, and Christ's followers will be refined in the process (godly maturity through sanctification).

I believe that Satan's two most effective forms of combat against Christ's followers are deception and intimidation. His greatest deception is tricking Christ's followers into thinking that they are not worthy of witnessing, not able to witness, and/or not needed. In reality, all of Christ's followers are called to witness, enabled to witness through the empowerment of the Holy Spirit, and worthy of witnessing through Christ's righteousness working in them.[a] If you fear witnessing for any reason, ask God to give you discernment and empowerment. He will help you know when and how to witness in all circumstances.

Putting on the Whole Armor of God

God empowers and guides those who are listening to Him. Since the Cross, Jesus personally guides, protects, and empowers His followers through the *indwelling of the Holy Spirit.*[b] Jesus' followers from all Christian denominations need to keep their spiritual armor in good working order, properly fitted, and *on* at all times in order to see through Satan's deceptions and move according to God's will.[c] The full armor of God is supplied by God to all of Jesus' followers who stay in a good working relationship with Him. The Father Himself protects them as they follow Jesus through the ongoing spiritual battles. At times, God asks His children to give up their physical lives and come Home helping others to know Him through their sacrifices.

When Paul used the metaphor of putting on the whole armor of God in Ephesians chapter 6 as a way to be prepared to do spiritual battle against Satan and his accomplices, he wanted Jesus' followers to realize that they need God's help; *as long as they walk according to God's will, they have all the protection that*

---

a: (a) Matt 28:18-20; John 15:1-5; Acts 1:8; (b) John 14:16-17; Acts 1:8; (c) Eph 6:10-15.

they need. Like a good soldier putting on each piece of defensive and offensive gear in order to be prepared properly for battle, they will be able to overcome Satan and his schemes.

Look at Paul's list of pieces comprising the spiritual armor that all of Jesus' followers are to wear:

(1) *truth*, which makes up a carrying belt for all of their spiritual tools;

(2) *righteousness*, which makes up a breastplate protecting their vital organs;

(3) *preparedness to proclaim the Gospel of Peace*, which makes them effective witnesses wherever God leads;

(4) *faith*, which provides a movable shield to be positioned as needed to stop Satan's deadly thrusts;

(5) *salvation*, which provides a helmet covering their heads so that they do not suffer loss of ability to see, hear, and understand what is happening;

(6) *knowledge of the Word of God* through the teaching of the Holy Spirit and willingness to follow His leading, which empowers each with both an offensive and defensive sword in order to clear the way for truth to be known; and

(7) *continual prayer* at all times staying in contact with God through ongoing communication: listening and talking.

Living holy lives and handling the Word of God correctly through the instruction and leading of the Holy Spirit allows Jesus' followers to defend themselves against Satan and to overcome Satan's deceptive practices against those walking in darkness.[a]

Even if we live righteously, study God's Word, and follow the leading of the Holy Spirit, a holy life does not mean that we will not someday become a casualty of war. Like Jesus, our Heavenly Father is using our efforts including the loss of our physical lives for the ultimate building up of His eternal holy family and kingdom, which is also *our* kingdom and *our* eternal close-knit holy family. God will bring good out of every experience of pain and suffering that His children undergo.[b]

---

a: (a) Eph 6:10-18; 1 Thess 5:14-22; (b) Rom 8:28; cf. Col 1:24.

Heaven or Hell?

Have you ever wondered why God does not just take each of us into Heaven and show us around and then take us to Hell and do likewise, so that we might be able to make an informed decision of where we want to be for eternity? When I was young, I did. It seemed that manifesting the two would be an easier way to convince many to follow Him. But, as I got older, I realized that *God does not want anyone making a decision to follow Him based on things but instead on the eternal relationship that He offers all.* Although Heaven is going to be a great place to call home, a place that will make even the best places on earth seem mediocre, God wants us to make our eternal choice of family and friends based on a desire to live with Him in a truly caring community. If we do not submit to our loving Heavenly Father and allow Him to complete our transformation into His moral and family image, we have automatically chosen Hell for our eternal home.[a] What does Scripture teach about Hell?

Hell

> If an eye of yours causes you to stumble, cast it away; it is better for you to enter into the Kingdom of Heaven single eyed than having two eyes to be thrown into *Geenna* (Gehenna: Hell)[14] where their worm is not dead and the fire is not extinguished.
> Mark 9:47-48 (cf. Matt 7:13-14)

Satan has already made his eternal decision to separate himself from God and overthrow Him if possible. If Satan could take control of the Father, the Son, the Holy Spirit, and all who are associated with Them, he would. But, the good news is that God is not only filled with loving-kindness toward those who receive Him, He is great *and able to maintain control.* Satan cannot

---

a: (a) 2 Thess 2:10-12.

change what God sets in motion, and *God desires for there to be two kingdoms*: the Kingdom of Heaven and the Kingdom of Hell. God is insuring that He and those who choose to be part of His eternal intimate holy family have perfect love with its resulting joy and peace. He will *not allow* any disruptions in the *new* Heaven, but the kingdom called Hell will be full of agony, despair, unrest, and shame.

When we look to God's Word to understand the living conditions of the Kingdom of Hell more fully, we come away with a deeper desire to help as many as possible make it into the Kingdom of Heaven. Hell is a very disturbing and hurtful place. Once one is placed there in shame, he or she stays forever.[a] We learn from Scripture that those who are placed in Hell for eternity undergo eternal unrest and suffering that affects them both physically and mentally. We see metaphorical imagery depicting physical pain compared to being burned continuously by fire and an eternal worm devouring the flesh but never completing the task.[15] [b] We also see the pain of Hell as something similar to having just experienced the loss of a loved one who is very dear to you causing much "weeping and gnashing of teeth [Matt 8:12; 13:42; 25:30]." There are also other metaphorical images of general humiliation, shame, and discomfort including metaphorical imagery of sleeping on a bed of maggots and having a giant worm for a covering.[c] We do not have explicit statements regarding the pain, suffering, and humiliation of being eternally in Hell, but we have enough metaphorical imagery that shouts loudly, *"beware, stay out, pain, danger, and humiliation ahead!"*

When one rejects God, one's pain and suffering starts immediately after physical death,[d] while waiting in lower Sheol (Hades) for their final judgment in God's court at the end of Jesus' thousand year reign. All of the disobedient wait in Hades until the great judgment day. At that time, they will be formally charged and judged according to their actions,[e] which will include as part of their sentence the *second death*, which is total eternal separation

---

a: (a) Dan 12:2; Matt 25:46; cf. Rev 20:11-15; (b) Isa 66:24; Mark 9:47-48; (c) Isa 14:11; Dan 12:2; (d) Luke 16:23-25; (e) Matt 25:45; Rom 2:13; Rev 20:12.

from God in a place called Hell, Gehenna, or the Lake of Fire,[(a)] which burns forever.[(b)]

Considering terminology, most of our modern English usage of the word "Hell" in Scripture comes from translating two Greek words, *Geenna* (Gehenna) and *Tartarosas* (Tartarus) as "Hell." In addition to the Greek wording *Geenna* and *Tartarosas* used to express "Hell," in Revelations 19:20 and 20:10-15, the Apostle John used the terminology "Lake of Fire." First, we learn from Scripture that Hell (Gehenna) is not the same place as Sheol, which is an English translation of Old Testament Hebrew. When Scripture is further examined, we find that Sheol, which is called Hades in the New Testament,[16] [(c)] is in reality a jail, a place of waiting for the final judgment trial,[(d)] from which all in jail will be sentenced to eternal separation from God and placed in a prison called Gehenna, Tartarus, the Lake of Fire, or simply Hell.

Before Jesus died on a cross for the sins of all, Sheol/Hades was the place where *all* went when they died,[(e)] because everyone had to wait for the Messiah's atoning work. Until He came, all waited in either upper or lower Sheol.[(f)] Upper Sheol contained those who had come to trust and obey God during their lifetime while lower Sheol contained those who had not.[(g)]

We learn from 1 Samuel 28:7-15-20 that God allowed King Saul to interrupt Samuel's life in Sheol in order to talk with him about future events. It appears that King David had some understanding that God could and would raise some out of this temporary holding place in the future.[(h)] The prophet Daniel also proclaimed a future resurrection of those in Sheol with some obtaining an *eternal* life with God and some obtaining an *eternal* state of disgrace and contempt.[(i)] God gave further wisdom through one of David's psalms declaring that in addition to David's expected resurrection, God's Anointed One, the coming Messiah would be raised from the dead of Sheol without suffering bodily decay.[17] [(j)]

---

a: (a) Rev 20:11-15; (b) Matt 25:41, 46; Rev 19:20; (c) Acts 2:27, 31; (d) Matt 11:21-24; Rev 20:14; (e) 1 Sam 2:6; 2 Sam 22:6; Ps 88:3; 89:48; Ezek 26:20; (f) Luke 16:19-31; (g) cf. John 3:36; (h) Ps 49 [49:15]; 86:13; (i) Dan 12:2; (j) Ps 16:8-11; cf Acts 2:22-36.

The Old Testament writers knew of a range of depth within Sheol.[a] Jesus' account of Lazarus and the rich man's death and subsequent life in Hades/Sheol helps us understand that there are two major areas within Hades with the higher reserved for the faithful and preferred over the second, which was further down in the depths of Hades and reserved for those who had not listened to God and followed His way of life.[b] From Jesus' promise to one of the criminals with whom He was crucified, we learn that he was going to be with Him that very day in the upper area of Hades, which Jesus called "Paradise."[c]

The ungodly group is still presently waiting in lower Sheol (Hades) for the final trial and judgment. At that time, they will stand trial before Jesus and be sentenced to appropriate punishment according to their actions along with a sentence of eternal isolation from God, which is also known as the second death.[d]

After Jesus' three days in Sheol proclaiming the goodness of God and during His resurrection, those who lived in the upper area of Sheol, Paradise, were escorted by Jesus into His Father's presence.[e] Ignatius (A.D. 37-107), an early Christian writer and martyr, said that after dying on a cross, Jesus went down into Hades alone but ascended with a multitude having torn down the "middle-wall," which had been dividing God and man.[18] It appears from Paul's testimony, that after Jesus' resurrection, Paradise (Upper Sheol) was moved into an area also called the Third Heaven,[f] which God allowed Paul to visit and hear things that encouraged him, but that he dared not repeat.[g] Those who were trusting God prior to the Cross were made perfectly righteous through Jesus' atoning death and were then allowed to be in God's immediate presence. Now, there is only the lower level of Sheol containing those who are waiting for their trial on the great day of

---

a: (a) Deut 32:22; Prov 9:18; (b) Luke 16:19-31- the rich man had to lift up his eyes-look up- to see Lazarus with Abraham; (c) Luke 23:43; cf. Matt 12:39-40- Jesus will spend three days in the heart of the earth John 2:19; Matt 12:39-40; Acts 2:22-36; cf. Ps 16:10; Eph 4:7-13- cf. Ps 68:18; Isaiah 42:6-7; 1 Peter 3:19-20; Rom 10:4-13; cf. Deut 30:10-16; (d) Rev 20:14; (e) Eph 4:8-10; Heb 2:9; 2 Cor 5:6-8; cf. 2 Cor 12:1-4; (f) 2 Cor 12:4; cf. Luke 23:43; (g) 2 Cor 12:1-6.

judgment, which is coming to all who reject God and His way of life.[a]

The New Heaven

> I heard a great voice coming from the Throne
> saying, "Behold, the dwelling of the [one true] God
> is with the [saved] people, and He shall dwell with
> them, and they shall be His people, and He shall
> wipe away every tear from their eyes, and death
> shall be no more, nor sorrow, nor weeping, nor
> suffering shall be any more; the first things have
> passed."   Rev 21:3-4[b]

Peter said that the god (sustainer) and father of our Lord Jesus Christ deserves to be blessed by all. He said that it was God the Father who has caused Jesus' followers to be spiritually born, justified, and glorified. It was God's righteous work that made it possible for those who lived their life trusting God to have an imperishable inheritance in Heaven.[c] So, what do we know about the New Heaven from Scripture?

Although He does not give a lot of detail about the New Heaven and the New Jerusalem, God gives enough information to inform all that it will make even the very best on earth of any age seem mediocre. Have you ever visited a city suspended in space or sitting on part of the earth that extends vertically 1500 miles high? With our present limitations, we feel that we are doing good to build buildings that extend upward one quarter to one half mile.[19] But what about building a city that shows the glory of God in its dazzling splendor starting with its size?[d] It is 1500 miles wide, 1500 miles deep, and 1500 miles high. That is the outer dimensions of the New Jerusalem![e] This city is home for all of God's children in Heaven with its gates open all of the time in an

---

a: (a) Rev 20:11-13-15; (b) cf. Rev 21:1; 2 Peter 3:10-13; Isa 66:22; consider Rom 8:18-23; (c) 1 Peter 1:3-5; Rev 12:7; John 3:5; Rom 1:16-17; 8:30; (d) Rev 21:11; (e) Rev 21:2, 16.

eternal state of peace within Heaven.[a] The walls of the city consisting of jasper have twelve foundations made of precious gems while much of the city including its streets are made of pure translucent gold.[b] The city has three gates on each of its four sides individually made of gigantic pearl material.[c] There will be no lights, because God's radiance will illuminate everything and the Sacrificial Lamb will be its central source of light.[d] Wow!

The Relational Aspect of Heaven

. . . For *our citizenship exists in Heaven* from which we are awaiting a savior, the lord Jesus Christ, who *shall transform our body* of lowly nature *into a similar form to the body of His glory* according to the effective working of His ability and the subjecting of all things to Himself.   Phil 3:20-21

Beloved, *right **now** we are children of God*, and it has not yet been manifested what we shall be like. (But), we know that when He is manifested, we shall be like Him because we shall see Him just as He is.   1 John 3:2

Now, what about God's desired relationship with us? We know that God has created us to be part of His eternal mature loving righteous close-knit family, and if we receive Him into our lives as **both lord and savior**, God's desire becomes reality for us. God has created each of us to be an intimate family member experiencing perfect love, peace, and joy with Him forever.

In Jesus' personal revelation to John for His followers, we take note that in our future New Heaven, our Heavenly Father is *with* His children.[e] He does not distance Himself in any way from His children, but instead, He is right in the midst of His family.

---

a: (a) Rev 21:25; (b) Rev 21:18-21; (c) Rev 21:21; (d) Rev 21:23; 22:5; (e) Rev 21:3.

Each individual who learns to trust the Father and Son will be transformed into the likeness of the Father's very nature.[a]

Part of being like Jesus–with similar resurrected bodies–means that the miracle of Jesus' death on the Cross will become reality for all who learn to trust God from the beginning of time right up to the final judgment.[b] In Heaven, all sin has been removed along with any propensity to sin.[c] Without sin in Heaven, there will be no more unrest, pain, sorrow, and death.[d] God's children will drink from the Water of Life and eat from the Tree of Life abundantly.[e]

When Jesus prayed the night before He died on the Cross as the Savior of the World, we should take special note of the fact that He stated that *He was sharing His glory with all who were and would be trusting in Him.* Through His desire to share His sonship and personal attributes with His followers,[f] He was insuring our close-knit holy unity. All who become part of God's holy family are guaranteed perfect unity with the Father, the Son, the Holy Spirit, and all other eternal holy family members.[g]

When we look at Jesus' journey of life for our salvation, it becomes apparent that He went through three changes in the process of saving us. *First*, the Father and He worked out a transformation from the purely spiritual to the physical realm.[h] The Son, who had been identical to the Father in nature and make-up, now took on a purely physical lower form of life[i] culminating in His death on everyone's behalf.[j] This was a joint venture of the Father, Son, and Holy Spirit that allowed God to speak to us face-to-face.[k] A *second* change occurred after suffering humiliation, a terrible beating, and suffocation on a cross. Jesus in a fallen spiritual state due to taking on the sins of all who were being saved suffered separation from His Heavenly Father in Sheol as punishment.[l] Then came the *third* change: after three days in Sheol, the Father raised Jesus up in a newness of life cleansed of

---

a: (a) Phil 3:20-21; Rom 8:29; (b) Heb 10:10-14; cf. 1 Peter 3:18;
(c) Rom 6:22; 8:28-30; (d) Rev 21:4; 22:3; cf. Rom 8:20-23; (e) Rev
21:6; 22:1-2; (f) John 1:14; 20:17; (g) John 17:22-23; (h) spirit & truth:
John 1:1-2; 4:24; incarnation: 1:14; (i) Phil 2:5-8; John 1:14a; (j) John
3:14-17; 20:17; (k) John 14:9; (l) Isaiah 53; Matt 12:39-40; Heb 2:9;
Acts 2:22-36.

all of *our* sin[a] in a new resurrected spiritual-physical form. After suffering for all humanity, Jesus would never die again.[b] Jesus took on *the completed state of the Creation,*[c] *a perfected spiritual-physical humanity*, and now is working to bring as many as learn to love, trust, and obey God into Their family to be eventually completed in a similar spiritual-physical state.[d]

In Jesus' spiritual-physical nature after the resurrection,[e] we note that Jesus could walk through walls,[f] He could change His appearance,[g] people could touch His body and feel substance,[h] He could eat food,[i] and He could ascend in that body from this physical realm into the very presence of His spiritual Heavenly Father.[j] The capabilities of the resurrected body are awesome working within both the spiritual and physical realms. All who faithfully follow Jesus will have a similar resurrected body with their own unique personal features. They will have the same abilities to operate in both a material and spiritual world simultaneously within the New Heaven and on the New Earth.

This is why we are going to be able to be an intimate part of God's family. God has promised those who follow Jesus that they will be transformed into the same state as Jesus' final spiritual-physical form. Nothing will divide God's obedient children. As socially responsible family members, each will take on their assigned responsibilities and corresponding authority.[k]

This is why the New Heaven is going to be so great. Have you ever considered what it would be like to live somewhere where everyone loved you to the point that you did not ever have to worry about somebody trying to hurt you spiritually, mentally, or physically? In addition, we will not be hiding from God because of anything that we had done wrong in the past that might produce shame because sin has been removed. We will become fully transparent no longer being afraid of what others might do in the future to hurt us, and we will joyfully serve one another as we take on our assigned responsibilities. We will all be serving one another

---

a: (a) 1 John 2:1-2, 29; 3:5; (b) Heb 6:20; 7:24-25; (c) Col 1:15-18; (d) Phil 3:20-21; 1 John 3:1-2; (e) 1 Cor 15:1-9; (f) John 20:19, 26; (g) Luke 24:13-35; Mark 16:12; (h) Luke 24:39; Matt 28:9; John 20:17; (i) Luke 24:41-43; John 21:12-15; (j) Acts 1:9; (k) Rev 3:21.

in perfected unbiased love for all without any sin under the lordship of the Father and Son. We will be living in a world where our Heavenly Father and Eldest Brother have saved us from the bondage and corruption of sin in order that we may experience a perfect life of love, joy, and peace with Them and one another.[a]

Heaven is going to be great–not because of how great the physical and spiritual realm will be–but because we will finally be able to know God perfectly[b] and be in His presence forever. At this point in time, we can only imagine what it will be like to speak in casual meaningful conversations with our Heavenly Father, Jesus Christ, the Holy Spirit, and all who have obediently listened to God over the ages. *Although it seems too good to be true, those of us who are following Jesus are looking forward to that day when we will actually realize our close relationship with God and one another.*

For those of you who have not really committed to following Jesus up to this point in your life, I encourage you to journey with me a little further and seriously consider following Jesus. Although many who are not following Jesus know that something is wrong and desire something better, Satan has been deceiving them into thinking that things cannot get better.[20] *This is a lie!* God gives everyone multiple chances to turn to Him and obediently follow Him and His way of life. *It is God who helps people change for the better, which ultimately changes everyday life for the better.*

God is worthy of our submission. If you come to that conclusion and desire to become closer to God and become part of His eternal close loving righteous family, we will pray together to receive Him into your life prior to finishing this book. If you are already following Jesus, I pray that the rest of this book will encourage you to let go and give God more control over the things that He should control and commit to following Jesus to the best of your ability. When you do so, you will gain much more than you will give up, and you will start experiencing more godly love, joy, inner peace, and excitement.

---

a: (a) Rom 8:21, 35; 1 Cor 2:7-9; Gal 5:22-23; (b) 1 Cor 13:12.

4

Waking Up Spiritually

Right now, take a moment, close your eyes, and consider the following scenario. Imagine yourself on the northeast shore of Japan at Honshu on Friday in the early evening of March 11, 2011 when a nine point earthquake struck the region, the largest recorded in history. Just minutes after the quake settled, the coastal area was hit by a thirty-foot tsunami wave. You have been on vacation relaxing when all of a sudden the earth started shaking violently, and the buildings behind you disintegrate. Before you can get over the shock from the effect of the earthquake and respond to the screaming, you hear a great roaring sound, turn back toward the sea, and see a thirty-foot wave descending on you. What do you say to God at that moment? With imminent danger, would you be resigned to any outcome with a sense of inner peace, knowing that if you died, you would immediately leave your physical body and Jesus would take you to meet your Heavenly Father, or would you be overcome with a sense of hopelessness?

Have you ever had a dream in which everything happening within the dream felt so real that you were surprised when you awoke and realized that it had all been a dream? In a very similar way, when someone starts listening to God, he or she starts realizing that there is more to the world around them than meets the eye.[a] God does not allow us to interact directly with the spiritual world that is directly interconnected to our physical world, but He gives us awareness of it. Within our physical world, God encourages all to engage in godly social interaction as we consider choosing life with Him for eternity versus eternal separation from Him and all who will be with Him.[b]

---

a: (a) Compare Rom 13:11; 1 John 1:5-10; 2:15-29; John 3:19-21; (b) Rev 3:20; 21:1-4; 22:1-5.

Although we are not given the ability to interact directly with the spiritual world around us, those who listen to God are taught to understand that many of the battles that we personally experience are spiritually based and can be won *only* through His assistance.[a] The physical world is affected by the spiritual and visa-versa. In the present, we affect the spiritual world through our actions in this physical world including through our prayers as God and His Heavenly Host defend righteousness in both worlds. For those who listen to God, the reality of a future world that is divided into two isolated regions called Heaven and Hell becomes the main focus even as we live out our physical lives in the here-and-now.[b] *Our world is temporary, and the future sinless Heaven and sinful Hell are permanent.*

From the beginning of the Creation, God has asked everyone to make choices. Originating from Adam and Eve's sin of partaking of the fruit of the tree *of the knowledge* of good and evil, all are born into sin and forced to experience both good and evil. We learn from both and then must choose to obey or disobey, to follow God or continue in our self-centered ways. It has been part of God's creative design to give everyone a fairly large amount of free will in order to allow each person to decide if he or she desires to join Him and others in a mutual caring interactive righteous way of life. God does not stand over His Creation as a hovering parent forcing everyone to do what is right. Through the Holy Spirit's teaching, God works with our individual consciences and shows us the advantages of living loving righteous gracious (holy) lives with Him.[c]

Although God works righteously and graciously in our lives, many openly rebel against Him and His holy way of life.[d] Even with open rebellion and sometimes hostility, God persistently works with all not wanting any to perish but all to come to a place in their life where they willingly turn to Him looking for help in living a loving righteous life.[e] As God encourages everyone to know Him and His way of life more fully, many will not change,

---

a: (a) Eph 6:10-18; (b) 1 Peter 1:3-9; 2:9-10. Phil 3:17-4:1; (c) Rom 1:18-32; 2:11-16; and others; (d) Rom 5:8-10; (e) 2 Peter 3:9; cf. 1 Tim 2:4.

but others at various levels of rebellion including–some who have hit rock bottom–start willingly submitting to His authority because they start to realize how good He is and how trustworthy and able He is to complete the good Creation that He has started. They start changing from self-rule to seeking His leadership, which leads to a much better life now and forever.[a]

Today, some think that God loves us so much that He will not allow anyone to reject Him and go to Hell or that going to Hell will be temporary and just feel like an eternity. ***This is wrong!*** Without submission to God out of a developing love, people will be confined in the future to an isolated place, a prison, called the Lake of Burning Fire, Gehenna, or more commonly "Hell" where there is no contact with God and His righteous followers forever. ***What one decides while physically living truly matters!***

Choices Have Consequences

God created everyone with free will requiring each person to make decisions that have eternal consequences and does not force Himself or His way of life on anyone. It is clear from Scripture that God would like everyone to learn to trust Him and choose to live with Him for eternity, but He knows that many will want to live life their own way and reject His leadership. He consistently encourages everyone to look beyond themselves and choose a life of unbiased love, peace, and joy with Him and others who want the same thing. As we noted above, at the end of the Creation, God will place those who will not receive Him and His leadership into their own isolated place commonly called Hell, and they will not be able to lower the quality of life for those who have chosen to listen to Him and become part of His eternal family.[b]

With abundant free will being a critical element of God's Creation, it is also clear from Scripture that God gives everyone multiples opportunities (spiritual awakenings) to learn to trust and obey Him. When the Creation is finalized, our Heavenly Father, Jesus, and the Holy Spirit want the members of Their close loving

---

a: (a) John 10:9-11; Rom 6:22; Rev 21:1-4; (b) Rev 20:11-15.

righteous family to interact maturely and freely within the Family of God under the overall leadership of their Father.[a]

With such a high level of freedom within His family even on Earth, our Heavenly Father personally participates in guiding all who listen through a maturing process[b] that eventually removes all sin from those who learn to return His love.[c] As part of Their plan, the Father, Son, and Holy Spirit agreed to take on personally a major portion of the pain that would be generated throughout the Creation in order to achieve ultimately a perfect free will sinless family and world.[21]

Although the first individuals of God's Creation, Adam and Eve, went against Him and His commandment that instructed them not to partake of the fruit of the tree of knowledge of good and evil,[d] we would all have done the same due to the lure of knowing and experiencing the unknown, if we thought that we might come out better in the long run through the experience. What Adam and Eve did not know is that this disobedient act would cause much pain and sorrow for them and all of their descendants, but it was part of God's overall plan that would eventually culminate in a freewill sinless eternal family. Although God knew in advance that all of His Creation would struggle because of Adam and Eve's decision to disobey Him,[e] He placed such a high value on creating everyone with the ability to make important eternal decisions that He allowed such and provided a way to restore fully those who learned to listen to Him.[f] All of this was done so that God's Creation would come to completion with an eternal close-knit sinless family that would live together in mutual love, peace, and great joy in a spiritual-physical state that matches Jesus' resurrected state.[g]

With our great freedom to make choices comes great personal responsibility. It is important to remember that in order to become a mature loving-kind righteous sinless child of God, we must play by His rules following His righteous ways.[h] There are

---

a: (a) 1 Cor 11:3; 15:28; cf. Eph 1:15-23; Heb 1: (b) John 15:2; (c) 2 Cor 5:21; 1 Peter 2:24; (d) Gen 2:16-17; 3:1-6; (e) Rom 8:18-23; (f) Heb 10:10-14; 1 Peter 3:18; (g) Phil 3:20-21: (h) Lev 19:2; Matt 25:46; 1 John 2:29; 3:10.

some today who think that God's ways are antiquated, and therefore, we can reject the portion of His life instructions (commandments) that we do not like.[a] This is false! Keep in mind that all of God's ways are based on His eternal nature and are for everyone's good. We should continuously thank God for His patience in teaching us how to live holy lives giving those who listen the best life possible now and forever in all circumstances.

And as we discussed above, although God loves everyone beyond their present comprehension, He does not force anyone to become part of His eternal close-knit holy family, and He does not accept partial holiness. We must come to the place where we acknowledge past transgressions against God and others and seek forgiveness of such, which coupled with a growing love, trust, and obedience will result in spiritual birth into God's eternal close-knit holy family. Without God's atoning work on our behalf, no one is worthy to live in God's future sinless world, the New Heaven and New Earth. And even though it is good to belong to and participate in a local church, that in itself does not provide spiritual birth into God's holy family (salvation). God makes it clear in Scripture that we must receive Him into our lives as lord as well as savior.

As we read the Bible, which is for all generations, we learn that the way of life that leads to eternal life with God is sparsely traveled while the lifestyle that leads to eternal separation from Him is traveled by most because they choose to follow their own ways versus His way of life.[b] Jesus teaches that unless we receive Him and His way of life through a growing love, trust, and obedience toward Him and our Heavenly Father, we will not see nor enter into Heaven.[c] Through His parable about a wedding feast, Jesus warns everyone including religious leaders that God judges all according to their heart and actions. All are called at various times, but only those who come in proper attire are allowed to stay.[d] He concluded this parable by warning those listening that "many are called (invited), but few chosen."[22]

In Romans 8:28-30, Paul used the word "called" to indicate being born spiritually into God's holy family (chosen), which is

---

a: (a) Isa 40:8; Matt 5:17-20; Luke16:17; (b) Matt 7:13-14; (c) John chapters 3, 14, and more; (d) Matt 22:1-14.

based on returning God's love, resulting in total righteousness and glorification as brothers and sisters of Jesus Christ.[23] It is clear from what Jesus, Paul, and the rest of Scripture say in many places that God wants to help us change to be more like Him, which will produce the best life possible. Without a desire to listen to God, one will not be led into a transforming loving righteous (holy) life, which is often called "sanctification," that culminates in an eternal sinless life with God, other Saints, and the heavenly beings who stay loyal to Him and His way of life.

As individuals begin to ask God for help, some start to understand reality more fully through the teaching of the Holy Spirit. This helps them to see more fully the good and bad existing in the world, which in turn brings some to a place of wanting God's help to live according to His way of life,[a] which includes following Jesus.[b] Within the process of receiving God into their lives and learning to love and trust Him, the moment that they truly want Him to be lord as well as savior, God gives them spiritual birth into His eternal holy family.[c]

Jesus taught that even some of those who called Him "lord" would not be in Heaven because they were not trying to do the will of His Father,[d] and therefore, in reality, did not have a relationship with Him.[e] He followed this teaching with a parable that taught the importance of having a strong foundation for life, which is God and His way of life. If we want a life with lasting love, joy, and inner peace, our life foundation needs to be God and His way of life.[f] This is why Jesus warns everyone that if they are not willing to listen to Him they are not worthy to be His followers.[g] Everyone who desires to be a member of God's eternal holy family must willingly follow His leadership starting at some point during one's physical life.[24] [h]

In reality, there are no "do overs." The writer of Hebrews said that it is appointed for each of us to *die once* and then *a judgment* will follow.[i] *There is no reincarnation!* All people live

---

a: (a) John 4:34; 8:31b-32; (b) Luke 14:26-33; (c) John 1:11-13; Rev 3:20; Eph 1:13-14; (d) Matt 7:21; cf. 12:50; (e) Matt 7:23; (f) Matt 7:24-27; (g) Luke 14:27; cf. Matt 10:38; (h) Luke 14:26; (i) Heb 9:27; Rev 20:11-15.

this physical portion of their eternal life *only one time*, and all will be judged according to the way that they responded to God during this short portion of eternity.[a]

Although it may be hard to believe, the hardest part of life for most people is *just waking up* to the reality of the spiritual world around them. If we do not listen to God and allow Him to teach us, *our own personal desires are like little children's, They cloud our reasoning* blinding us to what is really going on (rationalization). In addition, Satan's deceptive work continually bombards us with all types of diversions and busyness.

Our self-centered desires along with Satan's deceptions and busyness combine to produce a mental and spiritual smokescreen keeping many from coming to know God well. At times, God breaks through that smokescreen and reveals Himself. *Through His revelation*, we come to realize how empty our lives are without a close relationship with Him and that He has many faithful followers working worldwide to bring as many as will listen into His eternal presence.

God brings bits of reality into all people's lives through personal revelation, evangelists, preachers, teachers, family members, friends, associates, and even strangers. In our modern world, there are many ways to disburse information including pamphlets, magazines, books, phones, computers, ipads, android tablets, radio, TV, and more. Through these various forms of media, God asks us all to study and reflect on His Word, the Bible, in order to dispel the darkness around, which helps us see reality more clearly, which in turn starts freeing us from the bondage of sin.[b]

Billy Graham once wrote about a young lady who had written him a letter telling him how totally miserable she had been in her former free-spirited life. She had been pursuing the sensual pleasures of this world but found neither inner peace nor lasting joy from such. Through God's guidance, she decided to go to a Bible study and stump everyone with her cynicism. Instead, God used that time to build an interest in her to read His Word. She began studying a Bible on a regular basis and several months later God

---

a: (a) 1 Peter 1:17; (b) John 8:31b-34.

brought her to a point where she realized that God really loved her and had a much better plan for her life than she had for herself. At that point, she submitted her life to her loving Creator. She said in her letter that after committing to follow Christ, she experienced a happiness that she did not know existed. She stated that all those sensual pleasures were traps that had led her to confusion, unhappiness, guilt, and near-suicide. Now she was truly free as she followed Jesus.[25]

One of my former seminary students, Dr. Greg Viehman, tells through his book, *The God Diagnosis*, about some of his spiritual awakening moments where eventually God got through to him by having him consider the potential outcome of life if it were not eternal. Would he, his family, and all of their memories just become like the sand of the sea with no remaining evidence of the lives they had lived? [26] [a] After he had finished his residency and established his own medical practice, God started helping Greg understand the importance of repentance. On one occasion, His father-in-law invited a couple friends over to discuss the Good News with him and his wife, Ruth, and God gave Greg a supernatural peace about what he was hearing even if it was still hard for him to believe.[b] A few years later after moving into a new neighborhood, God gave Greg an incentive to study the Bible so that he might prove that his Christian neighbors were not properly following God's loving righteous way of life: Greg's two sons experienced sadness due to the Christian neighborhood children not allowing his sons to them join them in their play.[c] Because of his past experiences, Greg also focused on three questions: (1) why couldn't Jesus give everyone eternal life if He was God; (2) if Jesus was God, why was He crucified; and (3) why didn't God create many ways to Heaven instead of only one?[d]

After a fair amount of investigation into the Word of God including proving its historical accuracy, Greg came to the point of intellectually accepting the Apostle John's eyewitness account of Jesus and His atoning work.[e] He was now ready for God to give him a final spiritual awakening, a personal review of his sins and

---

a: (a) pp. 11-15; (b) pp. 27-28; (c) pp. 34-35; (d) p. 43; (e) p. 108.

the opportunity to ask God for forgiveness of those sins.[a] After
Greg received Jesus into his life as lord and savior, he was born
spiritually into God's family and felt like he had just awakened
from a thirty-six year dream, a dream based on deception.[b] Now
that Greg was malleable as a new creation in Christ, God started
molding him into His moral image. Soon after being born
spiritually and realizing that he was changing, Greg started self-
diagnosing and came to realize that through the work of the Holy
Spirit, his personality and spiritual understanding were improving
dramatically.[c] Then, as Greg started sharing his new found faith,
he discovered that many people, who were attending church on a
regular basis, did not have a saving relationship with God.[d]
Realizing that there were many people who did not have a saving
relationship with God, Greg wrote *The God Diagnosis* to help
others open themselves up to a deeper relationship with God.

There Are No Passes into Heaven!

If we would be honest with one another, most of us would
admit that we want things our way and want everything to be as
easy as possible. From what I see in God's Word, it takes
commitment and effort in order for anything to advance, whether
good or evil. From the side of evil, Scripture is clear that Satan has
been and will continue to work hard to overthrow God and His
children until he is permanently confined in Hell. He will not win
the overall war against God, but he is putting forth a major effort to
turn as many of God's children against Him as possible. Due to
abundant free will and high self esteem, he is doing well in keeping
many on a life path that leads to eternal separation from God.

From the side of good, Scripture is clear that God has been
longsuffering and working hard on humanity's behalf from the very
beginning of the Creation. The Son of God, Jesus Christ, working
with His Father even died both physically and spiritually[e] in order
to provide a way for good to triumph eternally. Through Jesus'

---

a: (a) pp. 116-119, 192; (b) pp. 121, 181; (c) pp. 166-68; (d) pp. 231-
240; (e) Spiritual death is separation from His Heavenly Father.

spiritual death on our behalf, He was separated from His intimate relationship with His Heavenly Father *for the first time* in order that those who were trusting God would never experience spiritual death even for one second.[a] Jesus provides a way to undo wrong and gives those who submit to God a righteousness like His own.[b] Any real advancement, whether good or evil, takes commitment and effort.

If all advancement takes commitment and effort, why do so many think that God, who is fighting on our behalf, wants His children to sit on the sidelines and do nothing? Everything in Scripture teaches that God's children are to be fully involved in living loving righteous lives and allowing God to lead them in their good works overcoming evil with good. Yet there are many people who claim to be Christians (Christ-like), who do not live according to God's holiness nor try to follow Jesus. These same people will tell you that *they are confident that they are going to Heaven when they die.* This way of thinking is totally contrary to God's Word. *Nowhere in Scripture does God teach that someone can come to Him, pick up a pass into Heaven, ignore the battles going on around them, die physically, and have Jesus escort his or her spirit to our Heavenly Father in Heaven.*

So *why* do so many people today make some sort of profession of faith saying that they trust God and either were baptized as an infant or after professing Christ as savior and never experience the new creation "in Christ"?[c] In reality, without a genuine commitment *to follow* Jesus Christ, there will be no spiritual birth into God's holy family nor corresponding new creation.

Today, there are many who believe that salvation is nothing more than asking God for a pass into Heaven to use when one dies. This lie causes some people to think that they have to wait until they get to Heaven before anything gets better. *What a lie! Being molded and shaped by God (sanctification) and doing His assigned good works starts immediately for all who truly start following Jesus.*[d]

---

a: (a) John 11:25-26; Eph 4:8-10; Heb 2:9-11; (b) Gal 3:13-14; 2 Cor 5:21; (c) 2 Cor 5:17; (d) Rom 6:22 and more.

The idea of asking God to be saved from our sins without making a commitment to follow Jesus as lord as well as savior is as worthless and harmful as the lie that Satan perpetuated in the Middle Ages that eventually caused a major reformation among many Christians. At that time, Satan had perpetuated a lie deceiving many into thinking that they could pay church officials to pray for salvation for themselves and their loved ones including the deceased, thereby giving everyone including the dead passes into Heaven. The *new lie, which is being propagated by many, proclaims that everyone can ask for salvation recognizing Jesus as savior and thereby pick up a pass into Heaven without following Him as lord.* This type of thinking is hindering many from considering a genuine commitment to follow Jesus.

It is only through a turning from self and following Jesus that one is saved from judgment as a sinner and spiritually born into God's holy family. *Spiritual birth into God's eternal sinless family and corresponding renewal only come from God according to His will and His rules.* [a] It is only through spiritual birth into God's family that sin is removed and one grows in godly righteousness. God's Word is clear: *if individuals do not make a true commitment to follow Jesus, they are not able to be His disciples.* [b] From the Bible, it is clear that being part of God's eternal holy family is only realized through trusting and obeying God out of a growing love for Him. [c]

Satan's ongoing deceptions are worst than His first to Eve in the sense that her decision to disobey God did not condemn her and the rest of the world *eternally*, but many of Satan's ongoing deceptions are aimed at hurting people forever. Many of Satan's latest distortions have given many–including regular church attendees–*a false sense of eternal security*, which has encouraged them to live like the rest of the world not actively following Jesus.

When those who do not attend church on a regular basis look at many of our contemporary churches, they do not see a holy witness where godly love is at work among God's people.

---

a: (a) John 1:13; Luke 16:16-17; 2 Peter 3:9; (b) Luke 14:26-27; Matt 10:38; (c) John 3:16, 31; Rom 8:28-30; Rev 3:20; 21:7-8, 27.

Therefore, we are suffering from a double blow from Satan's present deceptions:

> (1) *many going to church are neither being saved nor growing spiritually;* and
> (2) many outside the local churches have no desire to know about God because Christianity appears to be a social club where people help one another feel justified before God through association but are no more concerned for others than those not listening to God.

This ungodly activity is a terrible witness against God by many who are claiming to be Christians. Satan's contemporary deceptions are being perpetuated more and more giving many a false hope that most–if not all–are going to Heaven. The ungodly state of many local churches in the US and Europe *is corrupting God's Gospel Message in such a way that people are not encouraged to find an off ramp from the wide-road leading to separation from God.* It is causing many to live out their lives with less joy and inner peace than God desires instead of being born of the Spirit and joining Him in His ongoing creative work, which produces a much more rewarding life now and forever.

Throughout time, various forms of busyness have been the worst barriers to understanding God and the spiritual world in which we live. It is critical that all of us slow down and receive ongoing instruction from God helping us understand our world better. King Solomon is a good case in point. As a king, he was very intelligent and stayed busy developing Israel, which included building up its cities and armies in order to protect Israel from the world around them;[a] but, he failed to build up his personal and Israel's national relationship with God.[b] At the end of his life, he realized that his busyness in the physical world was not very important when considered in light of eternity. He came to realize very late in life that the most important part of anyone's life was to respect and listen to God.[c]

---

a: (a) 1 Kings 4:20-28; 10:14-29; Eccl 2:1-10; (b) 1 Kings 11:1-13; (c) Eccl 3:14; 12:13-14.

God Is Always at Work

Part of the Good News (Gospel) is that God is always at work helping as many as will listen understand the reality of the physical and spiritual realms of this world.[a] *Everyone senses both* through what they see in the physical world and what the Holy Spirit helps them see spiritually,[b] but keep in mind that it is only through their willingness to listen to the Creator that anyone is able to understand the reality of the world around them.[c] Through God's help, everyone can potentially understand both the physical and spiritual realms.

It is sad that for most, God has to allow bad things to happen in order to get people's attention. It seems that when things are going well according to our way of thinking, we do not have the time nor desire to listen to God even when we are not experiencing the type of full life that He desires for us.[d] Yet, God remains persistent working with all to awaken those who are willing to listen. The Holy Spirit is always actively working in everyone's heart and mind. Sometimes God gets our attention during quiet moments, sometimes through miraculous events, sometimes through tragedies including near death experiences, and in many cases through everyday experiences.

Job is a good example of someone needing some spiritual awakening. He was a righteous man, who respected God[e] but did not know Him as well as God wanted. He–like the rest of the Creation–fell short of doing God's will perfectly,[f] so God allowed Satan to torment Job through many trials.[g] When the time was right and Job had commended his own righteousness long enough,[h] God introduced Himself in a very personal way and brought Job to the point of acknowledging his own sinfulness. Like Isaiah,[i] when Job realized that he had sin in his life, he repented and committed to following God's ways more fully.[j] In many

---

a: (a) John 5:17; 18:37; (b) Rom 1:18-22; 2:11-16; John 3:19-20; (c) John 3:21; 7:17; Acts 22:14a; 1 Cor 2:10, 16; (d) Rev 3:17-18; (e) Job 1:1, 8; (f) Rom 3:23; (g) Job 30:25-31; (h) Job 27:6; (i) Isa 6:1-7; (j) Job 38:1-<u>40:4</u>-42:6.

ways, although our trials are not normally as severe as Job's, our life struggles are similar, and God uses them to build our character and our relationship with Him if we will listen.[a]

Although the spiritual forces at work around us cannot be observed through our physical senses alone, some of their evil is discernable through God's illumination. If we do not allow God to work with us and illuminate the reality of the co-existing physical and spiritual realms, we remain ignorant of the spiritual battles raging around us as Satan fights to destroy as many as possible. It is critically important for all people to submit whole-heartedly to the lordship of the Creator. Within His freewill creation, this voluntary submission gives God permission to train and empower us to do our pre-assigned parts moving the Creation forward.

The greatest spiritual battle that every individual has to face is whether he or she will allow God to awaken him or her from the dreamlike state in which he or she lives. In reality, it normally feels safer and more comfortable to stay in this dreamlike state than to wake up. This state is somewhat like an altered state of consciousness wherein each individual has found a familiar place within a certain group of friends and activities to avoid the unknown whether good or bad. It could be compared to a heroin addict who escapes from his or her physical and emotional pain of this world. Once someone has been on heroin for awhile, he or she becomes addicted to and dependent on that numbed state with the result that awakening to a world without heroin, in which one experiences the good and bad of life again, is very uncomfortable.

Allowing God to awaken us to the reality of the existing spiritual realm that permeates and influences our physical world can be just as traumatic as getting off drugs. God consistently works with us to awaken us to the reality of our spiritual and physical world and the consequences of our ongoing decisions.

For those who listen, God starts them on a path within a much bigger world than first realized. Those who allow God to awaken them start realizing a need to reevaluate past presuppositions and make appropriate adjustments in order to realize a proper relationship with God and others. Their

---

a: (a) Rom 5:3-5.

consciousness of the true world starts shifting from one that had been very self-centered to one that becomes more and more in tune with God, His standards, and His Creation. God is bringing as many as will listen into alignment with His holy nature producing eternal lives full of love, joy, inner peace, and excitement.

For all who allow God to awaken them from their personal self-centered worlds and start learning to trust and obey the Creator of the universe, they eventually come to realize that:

> (1) life is truly eternal for all people of all time with good or bad eternal consequences depending on choices made during each person's physical life;
> (2) those who obediently listen to God immediately become part of His eternal close-knit holy family and are given assignments during their physical lives (good works);[a] and
> (3) those who obediently listen to God will eventually be fully transformed into Jesus' perfect moral nature and live forever with Them and the rest of Their close-knit holy family in Heaven experiencing continuous ongoing godly love, joy, and inner peace.

Born To Die Once

> Just as it is determined (appointed) for men to die once, but after this judgment . . . .   Heb 9:27

A long time ago, there was a king who wanted God to help him remember that he had a limited time to live out his physical life. It would help him stay focused on what was important in life.[b] Like all of us, King David knew that he had a limited time to live out this part of eternity. He wanted to keep a proper perspective regarding his limited time in order to live out this part in a way that was pleasing to his Sustainer.[c]

_____

a: (a) Jer 1:5; Gal 1:15-16; Eph 2:10; (b) Ps 39:4-5: (c) Ps 103:33-105:5.

From the moment that anyone is physically conceived, he or she has an eternal existence. Then, God begins developing those who listen as eternal holy family members throughout this physical stage of their eternal life. The Creation is in process and will continue bringing people into God's eternal holy family until the last day of Jesus' thousand year reign. During this time, everyone has the ability to receive the gift of the Spirit and corresponding eternal life through submission to God. If individuals will walk in God's ways (holiness) and follow the leading of the Holy Spirit, they will be born a second time. They are born spiritually into God's eternal holy family through the eternal indwelling of the Holy Spirit.[a]

In Scripture, holy writers have used various terms such as God's "call, choice, or election" to designate those who have been born of God due to their submission to Him. It is God's love that draws many to Him. God's Word also makes it clear that no one is allowed to bring character witnesses before Jesus to speak on their behalf at His great White Throne Judgment. He has perfect knowledge of everyone's inner motives and completed actions and exposes everything to the whole Creation.[b]

Born into Sin on the Wide-Road Leading to Destruction

As we consider God's Creation, we can make a few observations:

> (1) everyone was created as an eternal being without having a say in the matter;
> (2) everyone other than Adam and Eve was born into a world corrupted by sin and is living on a common wide life-path (road) leading eventually to eternal shame and pain with marred characters if they do not get off; and
> (3) everyone who learns to trust and obey God out of a growing love for Him will get off the wide-road and start

---

a: (a) John 3:1-8; Eph 1:13-14; 1 John 4:7; (b) Luke 8:17; Rev 20:11-15; cf. 2 Thess 2:10.

following Jesus as part of God's eternal close-knit holy family.

So, how marred are we, and why would anyone want to submit to God's lordship? God tells us not to love the fallen corrupted world nor the various ways of the world because they are not of Him.[a] He describes the ways of the world as based on self-centeredness versus a God-centered love for all. God's Word is clear: a self-centered lifestyle leads to eternal pain, unrest, and shame, but for those who *willingly* live according to God's will and ways, there is eternal life with God and inner peace and joy that starts immediately.[b]

Let's take a look at a couple of uncaring sons within the Prodigal Son parable in Luke 15:11-32. As we look at Jesus' teaching about a loving father and *two* self-centered sons,[c] we note three important points:

> (1) the loving father worked hard to provide for his family and workers. He did not live in the moment but instead lived his life based on genuine love in such a way as to bless others *over the long haul*;
> (2) the openly rebellious younger son was not concerned with others nor the future. When he became old enough to be on his own, he left home to live life in such a way as to experience as much worldly pleasure as possible not considering how that would affect his future; and
> (3) *the second son,* who was also highlighted in Jesus' story, demonstrated a certain degree of faithfulness to his father by staying at home and helping to maintain their land, but *was just as distant from God as the younger son* because of his lack of genuine love for others especially his lost brother.

In reality, Jesus' story closes with two lost sons, who have experienced love from their biological father and had not yet

---

a: (a) 1 John 2:15; and they will not last 2 Peter 3:7-13; Rev 22:1;
(b) Rom 6:22; (c) Luke 15:1-2, 11-32.

allowed God to grow genuine love and concern in them. One son came home repenting because of what his father had to offer, and the other who stayed at home was living legally within his father's moral criteria but not from the heart.

When Jesus closed this story, He did not say whether either son had a genuine love for their father or others. It is possible that eventually both–having experienced totally different circumstances–would eventually come to the place of allowing God to teach them to love others according to His standards. If they did not, neither would be allowed into God's eternal holy family. Allowing God to lead and teach each of us to love Him and others more and more is crucial to becoming part of His eternal family.[a]

In this story, note that Jesus is talking primarily to the antagonistic Pharisees. The Pharisees are known to be morally good and can be compared to many of our contemporary church members. Many church members today have fairly good morals but are lacking a genuine concern for others. It is a good and noble thing to follow God's moral laws faithfully; but without genuine love and concern for others, one is missing what is most important.[b]

How many of us, who go to church regularly and try to follow God's general commandments, have no real compassion for the lost? In reality, both sons' lifestyles were ungodly, and those following either life path have no place in God's eternal holy family. If we do not have a genuine love for others, let's ask God to reveal Satan's deception and our own self-centered desires so that we might make a heart-felt decision to turn to God and learn to love more fully. No one is truly a part of God's holy family unless he or she is allowing God to mold and shape his or her image into one similar to His.[c]

Jesus makes us vividly aware that the ability to know good and to do good comes only from our Heavenly Father.[d] He is the One who is good, and all goodness flows from Him. Therefore, we need the Creator to help us evaluate our motives for the things that we do. The only way to realize any true godly love, which produces

---

a: (a) Matt 5:43-48; 22:37-40; Luke 10:30-37; (b) 1 Cor 13:1-8a;
(c) Matt 5:3-12; Gal 5:22-23; (d) Matt 19:17; Luke 18:19; John 20:17.

inner peace and joy, is to live out our lives listening to God as we live according to His standards. God wants us to realize a good life and helps all who listen to Him learn to love as He loves.[a]

The Righteousness of God

But now apart from law, the righteousness of God has been manifested being witnessed by the Law and the prophets. The righteousness of God is (realized) through faith in Jesus Christ—for all who are trusting, because there is no distinction for all have sinned and are falling short of the glory of God—being made righteous (justified) freely by His grace through the redemption which is in Christ Jesus.

Rom 3:21-24

The Consequence of Sin

God teaches us through Paul that the Law was not totally effective because of our fallen self-centered nature.[b] In other words, our selfish desires are at times able to override the holy spiritual desires that God implants into our hearts resulting in sin and consequential death. Scripture teaches us clearly that the actual penalty for any sin, any act that disobeys God's instructions for life, is death, separation from God and His eternal intimate family. Although we have been created to be part of God's eternal intimate family, sin has separated us from that very family.

During Moses' day, God taught those who would follow Him that they had to live loving-kind righteous (holy) lives: lives that were distinctly separate from those who were not walking in His ways. Israel agreed to follow God and was commanded to be a holy nation manifesting God's true caring nature to the entire world.[c] They were to be a light to the world just as Christ's followers are today.[d] From the very beginning, God has wanted as many as are willing from all nations to join Him as part of His holy eternal family. God with His righteous nature does not allow the co-existence of good and evil in His eternal presence knowing that

---

a: (a) John 13:34; 15:10-13; (b) Rom 8:3; (c) Ex 19:5-6; (d) 1 Peter 2:9.

such brings corruption and pain.[a] That is why Scripture teaches us over and over again that God is holy and demands that we, His created children, strive for holiness.[b]

All Are Sinning

Because our Heavenly Father is holy and will not allow sin to exist in close proximity to Him, Paul declared emphatically that "the wages of sin is death (eternal separation from God) [Rom 6:23]!" He also stated emphatically, "all have sinned and are falling short of the Glory of God [Rom 3:23]." This was a change of thinking for Paul, who in his earlier years believed along with many of his countryman that they could live their lives zealously for God following the guidelines of the Law and be saved without the atoning work of the suffering Messiah.[c] The author of Hebrews made the bold statement that the blood of bulls and goats had been pointing to what God's Son was going to do and that sin had not been removed by Israel's sacrifices; it was only removed through the Messiah's atoning death.[d]

After his encounter with the risen Lord, Paul came to understand that he and many of countrymen had not really understood the necessity of God performing a costly miracle stemming from His righteousness to remove sin from their lives.[e] In God's economy, sin had to be removed like bad cancer cells, not covered over. When we begin to understand how righteous God really is and how sinful we really are, we can make this personal by joining Isaiah and saying with him, "Woe to me, because I have been cutoff (from God) because I am a man of unclean lips . . . (I know this because) my eyes have seen the King, YHWH (who is leader) of the (Heavenly) Hosts (who is holy, holy, holy) [Isa 6:5; see also 6:3]."

---

a: (a) Rom 8:18-23; (b) Lev 19:1-2; 1 Peter 1:14-19; (c) Isa 52:13-53:12; Rom 9:30-10:4; (d) Heb 9:23-10:14; (e) Rom 1:16-17; Phil 3:4-11; 2 Cor 5:21.

A Real Problem

Well, as we begin to understand that God does not allow anyone with any sin in His eternal presence, we begin to understand that we have a real problem. Sin causes separation from God.[a] We begin to understand that God is holy and will not allow *any* individuals who are sinning to enter into His eternal presence. *Sin is not acceptable! It is like cancer.* If unchecked it will destroy godly relationships starting with our relationship with God. Yet, we know that God has created us to be with Him in close proximity as close-knit holy family members. In addition, we realize that although God gave us the written Law through Moses as one of His many acts of grace, neither the Law nor our obedience has saved anyone because of *our failure* to live out the requirements of the Law perfectly.

To live in God's immediate presence, there must be *no* sin with its resulting destruction to perfect relationships. *We come face-to-face with the reality that without God's help, we would all face the second death spoken of in Revelation 20:11-15.*[b] Without God's intervention, we would all be separated from Him for eternity. Without His help, no one would be allowed to live with Him as an eternal intimate family member. There would be no eternal peace for any of God's people.

Justification: Becoming Holy Like God

As we reflect on our Heavenly Father's supreme righteous act of love on our behalf, the death of His Son, Jesus the Messiah, we come to realize that although the Father suffered great agony over His Son's rejection and death, both knew that they were making *the only way possible* for us to be reconciled to them forever. *Jesus' death was necessary* to remove all sin from those who learned to trust Him.[c] In God's economy, the penalty for

---

a: (a) Isa 59:1-8; Rom 6:23; (b) cf. Gal 3:24; (c) John 3:14-15; cf. Isa 53; 2 Cor 5:21.

transgressing others had to be satisfied in such a way that all sin is removed and eternally eradicated. If any of God's Creation was going to live closely with Him for eternity, *justification, being made righteous without sin, was required; it was not optional.*[a]

When someone becomes aware of God's holiness and his or her own sinfulness, there may be a personal desire to clean up one's life prior to submitting to God and His way of life. The problem is that without God's help, no one is able through his or her own sin corrupted strength to achieve *perfect* holiness. That is why our Heavenly Father made plans prior to implementing the physical Creation to provide a way to remove our sins and renew our character according to His holy nature. It is God's righteous work–[b] not our own–that ultimately has the ability to transform us into loving righteous (holy) beings suitable to live with Him and one another in His Heavenly Kingdom. Through the miracle of Jesus' death on the Cross, those who obediently follow Him have *all sin removed and are given God's righteousness in exchange.*[c]

Over the years, I have personally seen many continually reject God's invitation into His holy family, because they wanted to wait until they had their lives more in alignment with His or simply wanted more time to enjoy life on their own terms. No one is able to straighten out his or her life enough to approach God without God's help, and the Good News is that no one has to. God just wants us to desire to live holy lives and make a commitment to follow Him and His ways. He does the rest. *It is God who shapes and empowers us so that we may start living godly lives in the here-and-now.*[d]

With this in mind, let us consider again the meaning of reconciled sonship as described in Romans 8:28-30. Our Heavenly Father is telling us that *if* we learn to love Him because of His great love for us:

> (1) we are *called* (*chosen*) and He will help us to mature more and more into the likeness of Jesus with His great grace and righteousness;[e]

---

a: (a) John 3:14-17; 2 Cor 5:21; (b) Rom 1:16-17; (c) 2 Cor 5:17;
1 Peter 2:24; (d) Acts 1:8; Rom 8:14; Gal 5:22-23; (e) cf. James 1:12.

(2) we are *justified:* our sins are removed through a great miraculous work of God, who removes our sins making them Jesus' sins; in exchange for our sins, He has given us His righteousness;[a] and

(3) we are *glorified*, given full-sonship and eventual perfect moral character matching Jesus' sonship and character.[b]

As we learn to trust and obey Jesus out of a growing love, we begin to stand upon our Father's promises. As we walk with God, we start to develop a trust for His perfect plan for a godly family and corresponding peace and begin looking forward to the day that we will be in Heaven with Him. As we join God in His Great Work and allow Him to develop us over time, we come to realize that we will not reach perfection during this portion of our eternal life, but *we trust God to complete our transformation.*[c] As the Father continually softens our hearts and strengthens our resolve to follow Jesus more fully, we become more and more compassionate toward others. There is great comfort in knowing that in the not-to-distant future, we will have our sins totally removed and will be conformed perfectly into Christ's moral image[d] as we enter God's immediate presence where there will be no more pain nor sorrow.[e]

Spiritual Awakening: Coming to Our Senses

> . . . there was a great famine . . . and he desired to eat his fill . . . and coming to himself (his senses) . . . and arising, he went to his father.
>
> Luke 15:14-20

Have you ever sensed that God has been or presently is saying to you, "Arise my love"? God is constantly asking people and nations to wake up, understand the consequences of sin, and begin living holy lives with Him.[f] In Jesus' day—as in every period of history—many people stay busy building their careers and estates,

---

a: (a) cf. Rom 3:21-28; Gal 3:13; 2 Cor 5:17-21; (b) cf. John 1:14; 17:23, 26; Rom 8:14-17; 1 John 3:1-2; (c) Phil 1:6; (d) Rom 8:29; 1 John 3:1-2; (e) Rev 21:1-7; (f) Isa 60:1-3.

but too much busyness is counterproductive in developing relationships with the Creator and other people. As we discussed earlier, whether it is technological distractions, general entertainment, perversions, perverted relationships, work, or just busyness in general, one should not allow busyness to sidetrack them from listening to God. Through the Holy Spirit's work and Jesus' leadership, the Father uses His faithful people of every generation to help awaken those who are spiritually slumbering through personal interaction and all types of media, including pamphlets, magazines, books, radio, TV, E-mail, ipads, android tablets, and the list goes on. He also uses personal crises and other events in the life of each person to either draw people to Him or strengthen those who are already committed and following Him.

Initially, most people do not listen to what God is saying. They only ask God for help in fulfilling their own self-centered desires. This was true thousands of years ago through the many gods and perverted philosophies that Satan has used to deceive people. Satan gave them deceptive gods to help them with every aspect of their lives. Even today many people, who proclaim that there is only one true God, consider Him more like a genie who might help them with various difficulties in life, but they do not talk to God about building their personal relationships with Him. But, the Good News includes the fact that God is at work with all, and it is God who over time is able to bring some to a place where they start to care about Him, His ways, and their neighbors.[a]

Although people constantly ask God for favors, many do not really start to listen to the Creator unless something bad is going on in their lives just as it was for the younger self-centered son portrayed in Luke 15:14-20. Many people do not turn to God unless there is a special need, and then our Heavenly Father takes these opportunities to reveal Himself and teach the importance of caring about others. While He has their attention during difficult times, He works in their lives showing them a genuine need for His help beyond their present circumstances. He shows them the advantage of becoming part of an eternal caring family, the need for removal of sin, and how through His great love, He has

---

a: (a) Matt 22:37-40.

provided a way through Jesus Christ for everyone to become perfect and join His caring righteous family.[a]

For those who start to listen beyond their immediate concerns, God starts guiding them off the wide-road leading to separation from Him and onto their individualized tailored roads with Him. These narrow roads have been assigned not only to lead Jesus' followers into eternal life but also to guide them into the good works that the Father has for those who listen. God consistently stays at their side asking them to allow Him to be more fully involved in their lives.[b]

In addition to what God teaches everyone about Himself through His Creation as the Holy Spirit illuminates truth,[c] He asks all who are willing–whether committed to Him yet or not–to learn more about Him through the reading of His Word.[d] God has inspired each of the writers of His Word, the Bible, and it profits all who listen.[e] The Holy Spirit will teach *those who have a genuine desire to do what God desires,* and they will eventually come to know the reality of Jesus Christ and His saving work.[f]

If you have a desire to know more about God or have made a commitment to follow Christ, you should be reading God's Word on a regular basis and allowing Him to teach you reality, which if followed sets one freer and freer from self-centeredness and corresponding sin. Jesus promises that those "remaining" in His Word (*reading* and *living it out*) will know reality and be set free from sin in doing so.[g]

It is important to allow God to teach you from His Word instead of doing what many do: they read into His Word what others have said or what they want it to say to fit their existing lifestyle. Many people–who do not really want to live holy lives and follow God–either consciously or subconsciously **read into** the Bible what they want it to say, **ignore** parts that cannot be made to fit into their desires for life, and in general **do not allow** God's Word to shape their lives.

---

a: (a) John 17:23; 20:17; Eph 4:1-6; Rev 21:3; (b) Rev 3:20; (c) Rom 1:18-32; 2:11-16; (d) Deut 4:1; 30:15-16; Ps 103:17-18; 119:5-12; (e) 2Tim 3:16-17; (f) 1 John 2:27; John 7:17; (g) John 8:31b-36; cf. Rom 12:1-2.

Here is the crux of the matter: starting with Adam and Eve's sin, everyone starts out with some self-centered desires for themselves and their families without the proper amount of concern for their neighbors. Everyone starts out with some level of blindness not fully seeing the devastating consequences of their bad actions. To help overcome this blindness, *God gives everyone moments of awakening with its corresponding lucidity* asking each person to decide whether he or she will start obeying His Word and His leading, which leads to a better life now and forever.

During those lucid moments, everyone has to go through an inner struggle deciding whether or not they are willing to give up some of their temporary worldly pleasures. It is during these lucid moments that individuals realize that God has a better life for them, if they are willing to become part of His holy family instead of insisting on having things their own way. Many individuals, who stay focused on themselves, soon revert back to the old familiar less satisfying life and become self-absorbed again forgetting the better life that God had shown them.[a]

But, Jesus' true followers are new creations and are being transformed,[b] and they are learning to love others as God loves all.[c] When they die physically, *they do not need a pass into Heaven* from anyone–including church leaders–because they are God's children. Heaven belongs to God *and* all of His holy children.[d] When they die physically, Jesus will meet them as their spirit leaves their bodies and escort them into the presence of their eternal Father.[e]

Is the Cost of Following Jesus Too High?

It is difficult for many people, who are contemplating following Jesus, to start this journey, because they know that one must put aside some personal desires (dying to self) in order to start building a close relationship with God. God is asking

---

a: (a) James 1:23-24; Rev 3:15-20; (b) 2 Cor 5:17; Gal 5:22-23;
(c) 1 John 3:14; 4:16-19; (d) John 14:1-3; 17:24; 20:17; Rom 8:17;
(e) John 14:3; 1 John 3:1-2; Rev 21:3.

everyone to set aside some personal pleasure and ambition and accept His individualized path for each. For those who start following Jesus, their love for God and what He thinks will start growing along with their love for others. This starts developing within them a growing inner peace and joy.

What I have found over time is that many have difficulty in giving up present personal desires for a life of ongoing service in God's holy family even if that service leads to a more fulfilling life now and an eternally close life with God and others in the future.[a] For many, it just seems really hard to accept such an offer from God because of *the possible lack of immediate gain*. Even when they know that Heaven is secured by God due to His great ability and power over everything, many still want things their own way. They are not willing to allow God to reshape their character to become more and more like His nor wait for the finalized New Heaven and New Earth without its sin, tears, and sorrow. In reality, many consider a present life of following Jesus *too high a cost* to give up present short-lived worldly pleasures and ambitions even if they could obtain more joy and inner peace now and a perfected eternal life after physical death.

Jesus asks all to consider carefully the cost of following Him in order that no one start out on a journey that they are not taking seriously.[b] He tells all who are considering following Him that they need to put aside personal ambition, commit their lives to helping others know God, and follow His lead in a loving righteous (holy) lifestyle that will include some sacrifice. He warns all that if they are not willing to do such, they will not become part of His eternal holy family that prioritizes love for all over everything.

Personal investment of time, energy, and resources into the lives of others is part of God's plan for all. In order to successfully implementing God's plan, one must listen to Him and learn to love Him and others.[c] Returning God's love is contingent on getting to know and trust Him.[d] Trust in God is developed through obediently following Jesus and actively stepping out in a growing trust to accomplish His will for our lives.

---

a: (a) Rom 6:22; (b) Luke 14:26-35; (c) 1 Cor 13:4-7; (d) John 3:14-17; Eph 1:13-14; cf. Heb 5:13-14; 2 Peter 1:1-11.

God is pleased with any and all good that we do, but He is also clear that any sin in our lives that is not removed will prevent us from spending eternity with Him,[a] and He reminds us that all have sinned.[b] At first glance, this sounds pretty bleak, but we should keep in mind that God has created all of us to be with Him forever.[c] So, in reality, He values our choices and wants us to come to a place in our lives that *we actually want to be with Him—not for the things that He can give us or do for us as if He were some uncaring distant genie—but because of who He is*. God truly loves and cares deeply about everyone encouraging our godly development. God works on our behalf doing what is best for each.[d]

A Personal Testimony

What We Were Taught Growing Up

There is as good chance that you–like most of us–were taught as a child to work hard, get a sound education, and make a place for yourself in the world. As a child, I was told that hard work coupled with a college education would insure a sound career from which I would be able to support a family, have enough money for some leisure activities, and have enough to help our children get started on their life journeys. It all sounded good and seemed logical: work hard, learn a good profession, keep on working hard, and raise your family in peace and prosperity.

What We Learn through Living

As we start maturing, most of us find that life is more complicated than what we had been told as a child. By my mid-twenties, I had finished my military duty and undergraduate studies at college, and my wife and I were ready to raise our family and

---

a: (a) Rom 6:23; (b) Rom 3:23; (c) 2 Peter 3:9; cf. John 3:16- "the world"-all people; (d) John 15:2; 1 John 4:10-16.

follow our career paths. While in college and through God's grace, I had built a relationship with a business owner that led to a business partnership as soon as I graduated. Life was good and matched most of what I had been taught as a child. I had worked hard and was now ready to settle down taking care of my family, continuing to work hard, going to church on Sunday, and seeking occasional times to relax with family and friends.

But, something started to happen along my life journey that probably happens to most people as they live out their adult lives. God persistently and consistently helped me to understand more accurately the finalized world that He is in the process of creating. As I studied His Word and applied what He was teaching me, He helped me understand more fully His eternal plans for a perfect Heaven and a place of separation normally called Hell. I came to realize that being sentenced eternally to Hell was not solely God's judgment for bad behavior but also an alternative for those who did not want to follow His lordship nor His holy way of life, which is based on a pure impartial love for all. I become more and more aware of God's goodness and came to understand that even prior to the beginning of the physical Creation, God had already made a way for everyone who would live during the Creation to be with Him in His completed perfection, if they would become willing to return His love. As I began to understand God's way of life more fully and how good it is to follow Jesus, I started to want to please Him more, and I learned to start letting go of my childhood dreams and receive His much more fulfilling plans for my eternal life.

God Gives Everyone a Chance to Know Him

I do not think that our initial childhood dreams and careers make much difference ultimately in deciding whether or not God is worthy to follow. Some of us may start off without any real aspirations but simply desire to take care of ourselves and our families, while others may have high expectations of rewarding careers in an assortment of fields. Others may simply not care to engage in anything and may just start off drifting without any real direction. But, in all cases whether or not we have followed the

One True God from childhood, I believe there comes a time when each of us realizes that there is a living interactive power higher than ourselves and that something is missing in our lives, if we are not interacting positively with that higher power. This is because at various times, God interacts with everyone from every cultural and religious background from conception to physical death encouraging every heart and mind to follow Him and His way of life.[a]

For me after military service, undergraduate college, and within five to six years of successfully growing a company, I started to realize that success and a reasonable amount of money were not as personally satisfying as I had been led to believe. While I had been developing our new company, God had been developing me. I was becoming more and more concerned about others through regular exposure to His Word and the leading of the Holy Spirit, who encouraged me to minister to others including the homeless and those in prison. I started to realize that caring relationships with God and others was the only thing of eternal value.

As I listened to God, He developed within me a love for others that brought me great joy whenever I could help anyone grow in their relationship with Him. I realized that having a right relationship with God was the most important thing that anyone could have now and forever. As I personally grew in my relationship with God, I realized that He was inviting me to limit my business activity and minister more to others. He was asking me to let go of my childhood dreams and accept the good works that He had planned out specifically for me before the physical Creation started. I just needed to follow His lead. Although I had recommitted my life to following Jesus more closely at twenty-eight, it was not until I reached thirty-seven that I was ready to close my business and take the next step in following Him. Over the following years, I have come to realize that following Jesus is a journey that provides constant godly growth as we learn to trust and obey Him more faithfully day by day–many times in the face of adversity even from those around us.

---

a: (a) Rom 2:11-16; cf. Rom 1:18-32.

God Encourages Us to Know Him Well & Walk with Him

Over the next decade, God helped me to know Him and His Word more fully through continual godly interaction with Him, others, and graduate level Bible study. God worked in my life in such a way as to encourage my wife and I to move further away from what we had been taught earlier in life and to refocus keeping an eye on what He might have us do to help others in addition to helping family and friends.

The Bible teaches that there is a wide common road (life pathway) that all start off on and many remain on throughout their entire lives. This common pathway leads to an eternal life of shame, unrest, and suffering without God,[(a)] but there is a second life pathway that is less frequently traveled. It is for those who choose to listen to God. This less traveled life path (road) can be exciting and leads to great godly joy and inner peace. Each of our lives are distinct, and God has a perfect plan for each of us that no one fully achieves but some follow more closely than others. Although God does not call most people into full time ministry, He calls *all* to minister to one another. As we listen to God, He enlightens us helping us to understand reality better.[(b)] As we follow God's lead and introduce Him to others through our actions as well as our words, we are encouraged, empowered, and experience excitement, joy, and inner peace.

Prayerfully, reading this book and studying the biblical principles within will help bring more overall clarity to your life prior to meeting God face-to-face. As you read further, let's consider more fully the idea that God created everyone to be part of His volunteer intimate loving righteous (holy) eternal family, and let's consider our actions from that eternal perspective. In addition, let's remember that Satan continually distracts and deceives as many as possible so that they will not take time to listen to God and begin to understand how much God loves them and wants the best for everyone. Therefore, let's keep in mind that *now* is the time for the followers of Jesus of this generation to engage our

---

a: (a) Dan 12:2; cf. Matt 25:31-46; (b) John 7:17; 8:32-33, 47; 18:37.

culture and dispel the spiritual darkness around us. *Now* is the time for the Church to demonstrate clearly God's love for *all* through our actions as well as our words. Through our spiritual rebirth and faithfully following Jesus, may we experience much excitement, joy, and inner peace as we make God more fully known to the world around us.

5

—

The Extreme Intimacy within God's Eternal Holy Family

> And we know that for those who are loving God, He
> works all things for good, for those being called
> according to (His) predetermined plan (*prothesin*);
> for whom He foreknew (*proegnō*), indeed He
> predestined (*proōrisen*) to be conformed together
> (*summorphous*) into the image (*eikonos*) of His Son
> for Him to be the first (*prōtotokon*) with (*en*) many
> brothers (*adelphois*); and whom He predestined,
> these indeed He called, and those whom He called,
> these indeed He justified (*edikaiōsen*); and those
> whom He justified, these indeed He glorified
> (*edoxasen*).   Romans 8:28-30[27]

As we contemplate the initial part of God's Creation with
its enormous complexity, we might experience awe of God. Psalm
19:1 declares that God is great and the heavens are declaring His
glory. As we continue to contemplate how God interacts with all of
us throughout each's life within the Creation, we should be filled
with both joy and awe as we realize that those who receive God
into their lives are the crown jewel of His Creation; *everyone is
invited* to be part of His eternal loving righteous family.

The Good News of what God is doing throughout His
Creation includes the fact that those who allow God to be lord as
well as sustainer and savior will undergo a transformation process
(sanctification) and become more and more like God. They will
learn to care more and more about *all* people and to work with

those whom God assigns. Those who listen to God experience the joy of following Jesus as their love, trust, and obedience toward God grows due to His gracious unbiased love for everyone.

In this chapter, we will focus on the close intimacy of God's eternal righteous family that can only be realized through the abundant free will that God has given everyone. Understanding more fully how close you will be to God and the other Saints within this holy family should encourage you as you follow Jesus.

As you read through this chapter, I encourage you to allow me to show you some in-depth detail regarding God's eternal family. For some, in-depth study does not come naturally. But, in order to understand more fully the closeness of God's finalized eternal loving sinless family, I am asking everyone to work with me through this chapter knowing that if you do, you will be blessed. You will be encouraged by knowing more fully who you are right now in your eternal close relationship with Jesus as part of our Heavenly Father's eternal holy family.[a]

So let's get started! I want you to keep in mind that we can only understand some points of Scripture well if we take into consideration the literary and historical context of what we are studying along with the grammar. One very important literary consideration that we sometimes overlook is the importance of understanding how each passage fits into the whole of the Bible (biblical context). Normally, we start by considering how each passage fits into its local literary context (what is written immediately around it) and then consider how that fits into the overall written work (book context: letter, gospel, prophecy, history, etc.). If the passage has been written by an author that God has used elsewhere within the Bible, it is also good to keep in mind how this passage fits within the rest of the author's work (authorial context: John, Peter, Paul, etc.). Then, keeping in mind that all of

---

a: (a) 1 John 3:1-3.

the Bible is the inspired Word of God, we look at the biblical context seeing how the passage under study fits within the whole Bible. When studied correctly taking into consideration the literary and historical context along with the grammar, all parts of the Bible will work together to produce an accurate picture of God, His righteous way of life, and the final form of His Creation.

God Persistently Encourages Everyone to Join Him

At the start of the Creation, we see our Heavenly Father working with His beloved Son creating a people in Their own image according to Their own likeness,[a] who would be suitable eternal companions (brothers and sisters) for Jesus.[b] They would become part of Their holy family, a people whom the Father and Son could relate to, share their lives with, and join Them in their service to one another and other heavenly beings.[c] They are asking all people to join Them in a mature serving relationship,[d] which in turn provides great joy and inner peace. Having a good relationship with God and others produces good works.[e]

During everyone's earthly life, our Heavenly Father lives closely with *all* as loving parents often do watching over their children carefully,[f] but not so close that we do things because He is looking over our shoulder. He wants us to listen to Him through the leading of the Holy Spirit, who is working within our hearts and minds.[g] At this time, the Father and Son do not fully share Their lives with us, but They will in the future. Similarly, as adults, we cannot live on the same level of intimacy with our young children as we can with some of our adult children and mature close friends. To make an eternal, close, mature, mutually-

---

a: (a) Gen 1:26-27; (b) John 20:17; Rom 8:29; 1 Cor 1:9; Col 1:16;
(c) Matt 20:25-28; 23:11; (d) John 13:5-17, 34-35; 15:12-14; Rev 21:3;
(e) Eph 2:10; Titus 2:14; (f) Matt 23:37; Luke 13:34; (g) Rom 2:11-16.

interactive, and holy relationship possible, our Heavenly Father is at work in a special way developing those who listen. As we submit to God's leadership and holy way of life, He develops us daily (sanctification) encouraging us to love Him back and join Him in His good works waiting for the time that He will bring us into His eternal presence to interact more closely for eternity. In a somewhat similar manner, we patiently work with our children as they are developing, waiting for the day that we may obtain a close mature loving relationship with them as adults. The major difference is that we are happy if our children's sins are reduced when they mature, but looking down the eternal road of life, God insists eventually on total sin removal in order that we may have perfect love, joy, and peace with Him forever with no barriers (walls) hurting our collective eternal relationship.

Keep in mind that any sin disrupts harmony.[a] Our Heavenly Father promises all who follow His Son's lead that He will *totally transform* each person's moral character to be like Jesus' through the miracle of Jesus' atoning death on a cross. This makes it possible for the Father's obedient children *to enter into Heaven without any sin. What a miracle!* Because of Jesus' atoning death, those who listen to the Father will enter into His eternal presence without sin and its resulting shame; they will enter into Heaven with godly righteousness and glory.[b]

God Demands a Response

As we discussed earlier, although God wants a close relationship with all, He does not force anyone to be part of His eternal holy family. He continually works with all to bring as many as will listen to a place where they start to understand their ongoing

---

a: (a) Rom 8:20-23; (b) 2 Cor 5:21; 1 Peter 2:24; Rom 8:28-30; 1 John 3:1-2.

personal sin and have a desire to turn to Him for a better way of life (repentance).[a] When our Heavenly Father sent Jesus to live among us, He provided us all with an example of what His love looks like in action.[b] After His death on the Cross, Jesus became our *one and only access* to the Father.[c] If we learn to return God's love, we will also learn to love one another.[d]

As noted above, abundant personal freedom plays a critical part in God's desire for a mutually-interactive fellowship with us. God will bless all who listen to Him both now and in the future.[e] Although God desires and strongly encourages all people to join His eternal close holy family, He does not force anyone to do so. But, beware, a large amount of freedom does not give anyone a license to do whatever he or she wants without eventually costing them everything that is worth anything.[f] *God is sovereign. He has the final say, and He demands that we learn to follow Him and His way of life if we want to be with Him!*[g]

If we do not allow God to develop us into loving righteous social beings and remove our sin, He separates us from Himself and His obedient children forever. If we do not listen to God and learn to care enough about others to help shed light on His great work, *the initialization of the Creation . . . to the Cross . . . to the Consummation of the Creation with its new sinless Heaven and Earth*, we will not ever become part of His eternal holy family. Instead we will end up isolated from God and His family in a place called "Hell." Any remnant of sin in anyone's life would take away from the perfect plan of God that produces an eternal sinless life without corruption, sorrow, and death.[h] God will not allow any divisions and unrest in the New Heaven and the New Earth.

---

a: (a) 2 Peter 3:9; (b) John 15:13, Phil 2:1-11; Heb 1:3; 7:25; (c) John 10:9; 14:6; Eph 2:13-18; (d) 1 John 4:12, 19; (e) Deut 30:15-20; Mal 3:8-10; Rom 6:22-23; (f) Matt 25:45-46; 1 John 3:14-18; Rev 21:7-8; (g) Matt 5:18; Luke 16:16-17; (h) Rev 21:4; cf. Rom 8:20-21.

Being Born a Second Time, This Time Spiritually

It is clear from Jesus' teaching to Nicodemus that if one wants to live with God for eternity, one has to be born a second time, this time spiritually.[a] Jesus taught His disciples that no individual could be born into God's holy family just because they had been born physically into this world or because they wanted to be in Heaven with Him. In reality, God decides each person's permanent placement based on whether or not a person receives Him into their lives.[b] When Jesus told Nicodemus that our Heavenly Father loves all people so much that He sent His Son to die on a cross for their salvation (being made whole, sinless), He was telling Nicodemus that the Father's love is different than fallen man's: God's love is unbiased and available for all who will receive Him and His Son as they learn to trust and obey the Son out of a growing love for Them and others.[c]

With God's gift of great freedom for all within the Creation and through the corruption of our world through Adam and Eve's original sin and all who follow,[d] we are all born into sin rebelling against God tainted by earlier sinful generations.[e] Through all of the hostile rebellious generations, God has never stopped loving everyone and has provided sin removal for all who listen to Him.[f] When Christ entered the world through the conceptive work of the Holy Spirit becoming a sinless child (incarnate) in Mary's womb and then growing up to become a godly man without sin,[g] He showed everyone how to live out a loving righteous life (holy) according to God's Word proclaiming and demonstrating God's love through His actions including His voluntary death on a cross

---

a: (a) John 3:1-8; (b) John 1:11-13; cf. Rev 3:20; (c) John 3:14-17, 36; 14:23; cf. 8:42-47; love for others: Matt 22:39; John 15:12-15; 1 John 3:10; and others; (d) Rom 8:18-23; (e) Rom 5:8-19; (f) Rom 5:20-21; (g) Heb 4:14-15.

on our behalf.[a] Jesus has truly shown all humanity how to live out God's written Word in loving-kindness, full of grace and truth.[b]

Even during our rebellion against Him, God loves all[c] and gives everyone many opportunities to consider Him and His way of life. He knows that some will start returning His love and following Him and His holy lifestyle thereby choosing His better way of life now[d] and forever.[e] As the Holy Spirit makes us aware of our shortcomings in light of God's loving righteous nature, each of us must come to a place in our lives where we are willing to admit that we possess a nature that is not up to God's desired standards and therefore need improvement to avoid hurting one another. We must come to a place where we want God to interact in our lives to start transforming us to care more and more about Him and one another.

As one starts willingly receiving God into his or her life[f] as lord as well as savior[g] due to His love and trustworthiness (faithfulness),[28] [h] God shows that one more and more of His nature and desired lifestyle.[i] As a person gets to know God better and better, he starts to realize how good God really is, and his desire to please Him grows. At some point, this growing relationship with the Father and Son through the help of the Holy Spirit brings some to a place of genuine trust in God resulting in a second birth. These individuals willingly and joyfully submit to God's leadership knowing that God loves them more than they love themselves. God will always do what is best for them and for the rest of the world simultaneously. With willing submission to God's leadership, one is born by God spiritually into His eternal holy family through His creative work.[j]

---

a: (a) Isa 53; Heb 5:8-9; (b) Exod 33:18-19; 34:6-7; cf. John 1:14; (c) John 3:16; 1 John 4:7-19; cf. Rom 5:8-10; (d) Deut 30:15-20; (e) Rom 6:22-23; (f) John 1:11-13; Rev 3:20; (g) Deut 30:20; John 14:15, 21, 23; (h) John 3:14-16; Deut 7:9; 1 Thess 5:24; Heb 2:17; 1 Peter 4:19; (i) John 7:17; 8:46-47; Heb 5:14-6:1; 2 Peter 1:1-11; (j) Eph 1:13-14; John 1:11-13; cf. John 3:5-6.

Being Made in the Image and Likeness of God

After God had created all of the animals according to their
own individual kinds,[a] He created humanity in His own image
according to the likeness of His own nature.[b] Scripture proclaims
to everyone that our Heavenly Father working with His beloved
Son created a people in Their own image (*be-tsalmē-nu*; "in the
image of us") according to Their own likeness (*ki-demutē-nu*,
"according to the likeness of us").[29] [c] This wording informs us that
Adam was created in Their image and likeness, which comes out of
a descriptive Hebrew word consisting of three parts (preposition,
main noun, and possessive pronoun), "in the image of Us
according to the likeness of Us," with "Us" referring to the Father,
Son, and Holy Spirit.

Just as the Son of God has been granted great free will by
our Heavenly Father–even concerning critical issues such as taking
on humanity's sin and dying in man's place in order to produce a
sinless family–[d] humanity was created with an abundant free will.
Not being bound by time and knowing that everyone would
initially rebel against Him, God still insisted that all go through the
pain and corruption caused by bad choices and learn to desire a
righteous life based on genuine concern for all or live forever
separated from those who do. Although our Heavenly Father knew
that this freedom would initially bring about corruption and chaos,
His desire for a ***mutually-interactive*** loving mature holy eternal
family led Him to choose this creative process to provide
ultimately a sinless family through the atoning death of His Son.
The Father and Son knew in advance the cost of this freewill
righteous volunteer family and were willing to do what it took to

---

a: (a) species: Gen 1:24-25; (b) Gen 1:26-27; cf. 3:22; Acts 17:22-34;
James 3:9; (c) Gen 1:26-27; (d) Matt 26:36-46; Mark 14:32-42; Luke
22:44-44; cf. John 4:34; 6:38.

produce it. After much pain and suffering, all will be made right by Them for all who learn to return Their love and follow Their leadership.[a] Even with the pain produced by abundant free will, God considers His Creation with its perfected outcome as *tov meod*, "exceedingly good."[b]

Brothers and Sisters

One day when Jesus was teaching about the Kingdom of God, someone came to Him and told Him that His mother and brothers were outside and wanted to speak to Him. This became an opportune time to teach those around Him about the closeness of God's eternal holy family. Jesus asked the one who had made the request on behalf of His biological family who His mother and brothers were. He then proceeded to answer His own question by stretching out His hand toward His disciples and saying, "Behold, my mother and my brothers! *For whoever will do the will of my Father in Heaven, he is my brother and sister and mother* [Matt 12:49b-50; cf. Luke 8:19-21]."

With this teaching, Jesus wanted those who were present and all future disciples to reconsider the idea of family. Although our biological families are normally closer than any other earthly relationships, Christ's followers are in reality closer to God and one another than any earthly biological family relationship. Yes, we all have a God-given responsibility to take care of our immediate family members,[c] but Jesus is teaching all who listen that His Heavenly Father is the head of all and that His followers comprise a very close-knit loving righteous (holy) family that is closer than relatives within one's direct blood line. *Jesus is so close to each of His followers that whenever someone does*

---

a: (a) Rom 8:18-23; 2 Cor 5:21; Rev 21:1-4; (b) Gen 1:31; (c) 1 Tim 5:8.

something good or bad toward any of them, they are also doing it directly for or against Him.[a]

The Completed Family of God

This close loving righteous family unity is far superior to even the best family unity on earth due to our present less than perfect nature that struggles to live in righteousness. Ultimately, God's eternal holy family members will love one another with perfect unbiased love loving God and one another as God loves us.[b] Keep in mind that on earth, there are millions of small family units. This is not so in the New Heaven. The small family units will be gone, and there will be one God and Father of all and only one holy Family of God.[c] Jesus said that in Heaven there would be no marriages, but instead, the Father's children would be like the angels in this regard.[d] When the Creation is complete, there is no longer a need to reproduce. God's eternal holy family will be complete.[e] The present function of creating additional children for God's eternal sinless family through small family units will cease.

Adoption: Our Legal Status as Sons of God

He came unto His own, and His own did not receive Him. *But, as many as did receive Him, He gave to them authority to be children of God*, to those who were believing/trusting in His name.   John 1:11-12

The first point made in this passage from John's Gospel presentation is that the majority of God's Creation–including

---

a: (a) Matt 25:31-46; (b) John 17:23; 1 Cor 13:9-12; (c) Eph 4:6; 2:19-22; (d) Matt 22:30; Luke 20:35-36; (e) Matt 13:47-50.

Israel–rejected Jesus' presence in their lives as both lord and savior. The second point is that *Jesus officially declared that those who actually receive Him are the legal children of God*.

Paul, a skilled lawyer of God's laws (life instructions), lived in a world of Hebrew, Greek, and Roman culture and thought, and he used similar Greek terminology stating that Jesus' followers have the same legal rights as Jesus Himself. This is an important concept. In the first century Greco-Roman world, if you had legal status as a son through adoption, you had all the legal rights of a biological son.

In his letter to the Romans, Paul stated that Jesus' followers were children of God and *fellow heirs with Christ*, who eventually would be glorified with Him. They were eagerly waiting for the realization of their *huiothesia*, "adoption as a son," and the redemption of their bodies, which is purification from sin.[a] In his letter to the Galatians, Paul stated that those who are chosen by God are received into His eternal holy family through *huiothesia*, "adoption as a son [Gal 4:4-6]." In Ephesians, Paul stated that prior to the physical implementation of the Creation according to God's loving-kindness, He predestined each of those whom He called to *huiothesia*, "adoption as a son," through Jesus Christ.[b] We also learn from Paul that those who are called by God are those who learn to return His love.[c]

Although Paul used adoption language in many of his letters when discussing Jesus' relationship with His followers, in a key passage regarding the sanctification, justification, and glorification of Christ's followers,[d] he used a common Greek term of his day, *adelphois*, to express the idea that Jesus' followers were His "brothers"–see my translation at the beginning of this chapter. During Jesus' ascension from Hades (His resurrection), He told Mary Magdalene to go to His "brothers" and tell them that He was

---

a: (a) Rom 8:15-17, 23; (b) Eph 1:3-6; 2:4-7; (c) Rom 8:28; cf. James 2:5; (d) Rom 8:28-30.

ascending to His father, who was also their father, and His god (lord and sustainer), who was also their god (lord and sustainer).[a] In Heaven, God's children, both male and female, are equal beings having assigned responsibilities and authority dependent on earthly faithfulness to God; on this level, they are all sons.[30] [b]

Oneness: Extreme Intimacy with God and One Another

> And not concerning these alone (immediate disciples) am I asking, but even *concerning those who are and will be trusting (peri tōn pisteuontōn)* in me through their word/message, in order that all of them *may be one* (*hen*) just as you, Father, are *in/with* (*en*) me and I am *in/with* (*en*) you, in order that even they may be *in/with* (*en*) us, with the result that the world may believe that you sent me. And the *glory (doxan)* that you have given to me, **I have given to them in order that they may be one** (*hen*) **just as we are one** (*hen*): I in them and you in me in order that they may be made complete into one (*hen*) with the result that the world may know that you sent me and that *you love them just as you love me*." John 17:20-23

The night prior to Jesus' crucifixion, He prayed aloud to His Heavenly Father so that everyone would know that He was asking that His eternal holy brothers and sisters have the same close unity with Him, His Father, and one another that He had always had. In agreement with His Father,[c] Jesus was asking that

a: (a) John 20:17; (b) Matt 5:9; Luke 20:34-36; Rom 8:14, 19; Gal 3:26; (c) John 5:30.

His finalized family coming out of the Creation would have as close a relationship with Them and one another that He had always experienced with His Father. Jesus starts this part of His prayer saying, "And not concerning these alone (immediate disciples) am I asking, but even *concerning those who are and will be trusting* (*peri tōn pisteuontōn*) in me through their word/message [John 17:20]." When Jesus started this portion of His prayer, asking on behalf of all people who learn to trust Him, He is helping us understand that through this Creation, His requested godly unity for God's expanded holy family is open for all who learn to trust and listen obediently to Him and the Father.

Jesus continued praying, "in order that all of them may be one (*hen ōsin*) just as you, Father, are in/with (*en*) me and I am in/with (ἐν, *en*) you, in order that even they may be in/with (*en*) us, with the result that the world may believe that you sent me [John 17:21]." When Jesus prayed that all present and future disciples may be "one," (*hen*: *a close unity*) with God and one another, He illuminates what it means to be saved and have eternal life with God. Jesus is praying for all who learn to trust and obey Him out of love[a] to be united in the same special way to His Heavenly Father as He is.[b] When we look to God's Word for a better understanding of "oneness (unity)," we are reminded that God said, "Let us make Adam in our image according to our likeness." The Father, Son, and Holy Spirit's unity is so close that Israel considered their God, which was written in the plural form, "our gods," as *ehad*, "one" entity, one God. *Jesus was praying that all who ever learn to love, trust, and obey God would have the same close unity that He has always had with the Father, which includes God's children being loved by the Father just as He is.*[31]

---

a: (a) John 14:15, 21, 23; (b) cf. John 10:30; 17:5.

> Jesus finished this part of His prayer saying, "And
> the *glory (doxan)* that you have given to me, **I have
> given to them in order that they may be one** (*hen*)
> *just as we are one* (*hen*): I in them and you in me in
> order that they may be made complete into one
> (*hen*) with the result that the world may know that
> you sent me and that *you love them just as you love
> me.*"   John 17:22-23[a]

This passage gives us the clearest meaning of what our
finalized relationship will be like with the Father, Son, Holy Spirit,
and one another. We come to understand that God's Crown Jewel
of the Creation, His Holy Family, will have a godly unity based on
sharing Jesus' glory, which includes His sinless love. Jesus is filled
with great joy as He looks forward to providing total sin removal
through His atoning death the next day for all people throughout
the entire Creation who learn to trust and obey Them out of a
developing love.[b] God's timeless love is clearly portrayed through
His Creative work at the Cross.[32]

Jesus Shares His Glory

In order to make this godly relationship possible within
God's eternal close-knit holy family, Jesus shares His glory with
His brothers and sisters. Earlier in this prayer, we hear Jesus asking
that His disciples be protected under His Father's name thereby
showing that His followers are *an intimate part of God's eternal
holy family.*[c] In addition to this request, Jesus declared a powerful
truth to encourage all who were trusting God throughout all time

---

a: (a) cf. John 14:19-21; (b) John 17:13; Heb 12:2; (c) John 17:11b.

by illuminating the truth of their present and future relationship with God and one another.

As we look at John 17:22, we see ***Jesus sharing His glory (doxan)*** and thereby making it possible for those who will return God's love to come into His Father's household ***with the same unity that He has always had with His Father.*** With the Holy Spirit, they share an intimate godly unity under a single family structure.[(a)] Jesus has provided a way for His faithful brothers and sisters on earth to be fully reconciled as His eternal sinless brothers.

The glory that Jesus is sharing with His followers stems from His relationship with the Father and His resulting character. Jesus is like His Father, who is full of grace and truth. As described in John 1:14, Jesus' glory is similar to His Father's glory as described in Exodus 33:18-19 and 34:6. Jesus' nature matches His Father's, who is full of grace and truth.[(b)] It is Jesus' sonship ***and*** loving righteous character that accentuate His glory and attracts individuals to Him much more than His intellect and/or power. His caring nature attracts some to Him as a multicolored spectrum radiating from a diamond in bright sunlight might attract some. God's children will also have a godly character similar to Jesus'.[(c)]

God did not create anyone or anything *for* His glory. God's glory is based on His eternal glorious nature and *is demonstrated* through His Creation.[33] His total character, which includes His attributes of strength, justice, and love, contributes primarily to His glory. Because of His nature, God is glorious! In Isaiah 43:7, the prophet Isaiah said that the way that God works with those who are called by His name and whom He has continually worked with, manifests His glory. Isaiah went on to say that those who are called by His name are His witnesses to the whole world telling others about YHWH's faithfulness, which contributes to His glory.[(d)]

---

a: (a) cf. Eph 2:19; (b) John 17:5; cf. John 14:9; Heb 1:3; (c) Rom 8:29; cf. Phil 3:30-21; (d) Isa 43:10.

The very nature of Jesus' glory is easy to miss if we think only in terms of power. A major clue to the specific meaning of glory within verse 22 can be deduced from the fact that Jesus is sharing His glory with *all* who follow Him of all ages with the result *that its quality enables perfect unity*. Gifts of the Spirit such as power, wisdom, knowledge, miracles, healing, proclamation, prophecy, and tongues would not in and of themselves help us form a perfect union and are not shared equally with all Christ's followers.[(a)]

The glory that Jesus is sharing with *all* of His student followers (disciples) *will enable* them in the future to live in perfect loving righteous (holy) unity with God and one another just as Jesus already lives in perfect unity with His Heavenly Father. Therefore, when Jesus said, "I have given them the glory that you have given me *in order that they may be one as we are one* [John 17:22]," we come to realize that He gave up His *exclusive* position as the Father's *only* son. Jesus is sharing His sonship *and* His Father's *nature of grace and truth* with those who follow Him. We recognize that the very essence of Jesus' glory, which He shares with all Believers,[(b)] is derived from His Father's nature.[34]

Jesus is sharing His character and position as the *only* son of the Creator with all who trust and obey God. Imagine how that would have sounded to the people of the first century as they considered how much more important it would be to be the only son of the Most High God in comparison even to being the only son of their greatest leader, the Roman Emperor, which would be extremely important.

If you lived in the first-century Mediterranean world and the Emperor had only one son, you would have had great respect for him considering both his present and future political positions. It brought great joy to all who were listening to God in the first

---

a: (a) Acts 1:8; 1 Cor 12-13; (b) John 1:14; 1 Peter 5:10; cf. Rom 8:17.

century when they heard that Jesus Christ, the only son of the Most High God, had given up His exclusive right of sonship and was sharing it with all who learned to trust and obey His Heavenly Father out of a growing love for Them. *Jesus had made a way for all of the Father's obedient children to have perfect unity with Them and one another. What a wonderful part of the Gospel Message!*

Looking Closely at the Meaning of "One"

In the world of the Old Testament and in Jesus' day, the Hebrew word *ehad*, "one," could mean a single entity, or a group of two or more people operating as a single entity. During the four hundred years leading up to Jesus' ministry and during the first century C.E., the Greek translation of the Hebrew word, *ehad*, "one," within the Septuagint–when referring to unity among God's people within the Old Testament–was consistently translated into one of the Greek masculine, feminine, or neuter forms of "one" (*heis, mia, hen*) depending on which form was needed for proper grammar. The Septuagint is a third-fourth century B.C. Greek translation of the Hebrew Bible. Therefore, we can confidently say that the meaning of the Hebrew *ehad*, "one," in the Old Testament and the various forms of *heis, mia, hen*, "one" used by writers within the New Testament all point to a close "oneness, unity" among individuals when used within the context of social relations.

We noted above that when God created Adam and then Eve, the Old Testament stated that they were created in Their image according to Their likeness (Our image and likeness), yet God was proclaimed to be "One" in Deuteronomy 6:4: "Hear O' Israel, YHWH is our God; YHWH is one (*ehad*)." This proclaims the "oneness/close unity" of the Father, Son, and Holy Spirit. When this verse was translated into Greek in the Septuagint, the Hebrew *ehad*, "one," was translated as the Greek *heis*, "one."

After God created Adam and Eve as male and female, we see Him saying in Gen 2:24 that they will work together in a close godly unity that we call "marriage" expressed through the Hebrew language as *lebasar ehad*, "one flesh." The Hebrew *lebasar ehad*, "one flesh," of Gen 2:24 is translated in the Greek Septuagint as *sarka mian*, "one flesh" just as it is written in New Testament Greek of Matt 19:5.[35]

We see from God's Word that when a man and woman commit to each other in godly unity (marriage), they are committing to work together as a close godly team versus agreeing to work together as two independent beings. They are agreeing to work together in a very close godly unity with genuine concern and overall love for each other.

As other scriptures are examined, we read in verses such as Judges 20:1, 8, 11, and 1 Sam 11:7 that when Israel was attacked by others, large numbers of men came out "as one man" (*keîsh ehad*) to overcome adversity and wrongdoing. This was translated in the Greek Septuagint as *'ōs anēr heis*, "as one man." The men of Israel came out as a godly close-knit team working together to overcome their common enemies.[36]

Another example of "oneness, close unity" is shown in Genesis 34:16 when Jacob's sons deceptively told Shechem and his father Hamor that if they and their people would become like Israel and circumcise their males they would all become *ehad 'am,* "one people" allowing them to intermarry. The Septuagint translates this part as *genos hen,* "one race" vs. "one people," but again showing that *ehad*, "one," was used to show a desired close oneness (unity) and was translated accordingly into the Greek word *hen,* "one."

As the Apostle John wrote to Gentiles in the common Greek of his day, it helps us understand Jesus' prayer for godly unity among His followers. We take note that John used the same Greek wording of the Septuagint corresponding to the Hebrew idea of *ehad*, "one/oneness." This helps us to understand that Jesus prayed for us to share in the same godly unity that He always had with His Heavenly Father and would again share with Him after His Father raised Him from dead.[a]

As John shared Jesus' prayer with others in the first century, they would have understand John to be saying that Jesus' death on a cross and the sharing of His glory would result in a godly unity for His followers that matched Jesus' unity with the Father. Through Jesus' prayer recorded in John 17, we have a clear understanding of how close we will be to God and one another at the end of the Creation in the New Heaven and on the New Earth. Through this same prayer, God's obedient children should also understand that they should experience some of this godly unity while living out their lives providing a great witness helping our lost World understand that God sent Jesus to die for all and loves His obedient children in the same way that He loves Jesus.[b]

All Are Equal: The Father Has No Favorites

There is neither Jew nor Greek;
there is neither slave nor freeman;
and there is not male *and* female;
because ***all of you are one*** (*heis*)
through Christ Jesus.   Gal 3:28

The relationship that exists between the Father and every true follower of Jesus is that of a loving Father and an obedient, *only* son. Normally, an only son in good standing receives a fair amount of favorable attention and full inheritance from his father. Regarding being loved as a child, our heavenly Father treats all of His *obedient* children *equally* as if each one were His only son

---

a: (a) Acts 2:22-36; (b) John 17: 21, 23.

loving each as He loves Jesus.[a] Jesus prayed that *the children of God's eternal family would all be united in close godly unity*: they would be "one" (John 17:20-23 [*hen*, "one"]). Paul uses the same Greek root in Gal 3:28 [*heis*, "one"; close godly unity]). *God does not have favorites.*[b] God has created each individual uniquely different emotionally and physically including such attributes as eye, hair, and skin color. *Although He has created everyone different, He wants all to work together in close godly unity.*[c] God's unbiased love encourages Jesus' followers to love all people equally.[d]

The moment that we fully receive Jesus Christ into our lives as our *savior and lord*—which means turning our lives over to the potter, who is our Heavenly Father, so that He can finish the good work that He started in us—we begin to realize our Father-only-Son relationship. Once we are born from above, it is a done deal.[e] Even in our present state of sin, we become our Father's justified children who are learning to be more and more like Jesus, who eventually will be completed in His likeness.[f] God tells us that when we have been born of the Spirit, He places part of Himself in us, His Seed, which is the Holy Spirit.[g] When we submit to God and His way, He begets us spiritually into His eternal family and we can no longer continually . . . continually . . . continually sin.[h]

As soon as we are born a second time, this time with the Holy Spirit uniting with us forever, we become part of God's eternal loving righteous family and our improving walk with God helps the World to see God and His great rewarding way of life more fully. The loving righteous nature and close godly unity between the Father and the Son makes it possible to know Both by simply knowing Jesus: when you know Jesus, you also know the

---

a: (a) John 17:23; (b) James 2:1-5; (c) 1 Cor 12; (d) John 3:16; 2 Peter 3:9; 1 Tim 2:4; cf. 1 Cor 13; (e) John 5:24; 1 John 3:1-2; (f) Rom 8:28-30; Phil 3:20-21; (g) Eph 1:13-14; (h) 1 John 3:9.

Father through Jesus' nature.[(a)] Where Jesus' followers are, Jesus and the Father are.[(b)] Jesus introduces us to a third individual who is united perfectly to the Father and Him, the Spirit of Truth. If you know Jesus, you know the Father. If the Spirit of Truth lives in you, the Father and Jesus live in you.[(c)]

The world continues to hear the Gospel from the Father and the Son through Jesus' obedient followers who are assisted by the Spirit of Truth, who is dwelling in them.[(d)] The Father and the Son *working together in perfect unity* have sent the Spirit of Truth, the Holy Spirit, to comfort and guide all of Jesus' followers. This is similar to the way that the Father sent the Holy Spirit to help Jesus during His earthly ministry.[(e)] *When Jesus asked the Father to give His disciples a comforter to replace His physical presence,*[(f)] *He was making this special Father-only-Son relationship start immediately for all of His disciples through the indwelling and empowering of the Holy Spirit.*[(g)]

Early Church Understanding

How did the Early Church understand the idea of Emmanuel, "God with us," and the godly unity that God desires for His children? Satan has been at work from the beginning of the Creation to keep as many people as possible from drawing close to God. But, he works even harder against those who start paying attention to God's invitation to join His eternal close loving righteous family. In his studies, Constantine Scouteris discovered that the Early Church Fathers had a sound understanding of God's desired closeness through the apostles teachings on Christ.[37]

---

a: (a) John 14:7-11; Heb 1:3; (b) John 14:23; Matt 25:40; Acts 9:4; (c) John 14:16-26; (d) John 13:20; 17:18; (e) Matt 3:16-17; (f) John 14:16-17; 16:13; (g) Acts 1:8.

Regarding Jesus' prayer for unity among Believers, Scouteris stated that the New Testament presents Jesus' followers with the possibility of realizing that *Christ's communion (fellowship/unity) removes in the most radical way any worldly communion*. Christ's communion is the creation of a new relationship, a relationship involving God and Jesus' disciples. He went on to say that John 17 has two major themes:

> (1) the godly unity desired by Jesus for His followers is not only for His immediate disciples but also for all future disciples who will learn to trust Jesus through apostolic teaching and proclamation; and
>
> (2) all disciples participate in Jesus' divine glory.

Scouteris wrote that these two points became a solid foundation for understanding God and His desired unity.[38]

From Ignatius' letter to the Philadelphians written around A.D. 107, Scouteris concluded that a radical change had occurred for God's children after Jesus' ascension: their focus had moved from a subject-object relationship to one of *participation* with God.[39] God had made a way through Jesus' atoning death for a closer relationship. In Origen's (A.D. 185-254) work titled *De Principiis*, one sees Origen teaching both the future perfection into a divine likeness and unity that Jesus had prayed for[a] and a present practical unity that expresses itself in Jesus' followers being like-minded in godly unity.[b]

In light of our early Greek Fathers, Scouteris sees God the Father as an accessible divine person who generates the Son and causes the Holy Spirit to go forth establishing a unique unity within the Father's kingdom. The Father has given of His divine essence to the Son and Holy Spirit, and in return they respond in freedom

---

a: (a) 3.6.1; (b) 1.6.2.

and love with absolute obedience to the Father's will.[40] He noted that the Early Church Fathers could now promote unity of God's people through the unifying force of Jesus Christ. In the person of Jesus, all divisions among God's children were abolished.[41]

Scouteris went on to discuss Gregory of Nyssa's (A.D. 330-95) teachings regarding the divided nature of each individual due to sin derived from self-centeredness. This divided nature due to sin deprived mankind of any possibility of living in godly fellowship with God or others. But, Jesus' self-sacrifice has the potential of reestablishing God's original desired harmony bringing those who listen back into a perfect unity with Him and others.[42] By becoming a real man with a concrete human nature, Jesus, who was of the same nature as our Heavenly Father, took on the nature of humanity and transferred godly unity to the human level enabling the unity that Jesus prayed for all of His followers.[43]

Having studied the terminology of being "in (*en*) the Father" and being "in (*en*) Christ" from a first-century Mediterranean perspective, C. H. Dodd came to the conclusion that individuals living in the first century would have understood this type of wording to denote a unity that transcends human unity, a close godly unity.[44] He said that Jesus' prayer shows a completed picture of unity for the Father, Son, and the Son's followers with love being the key. *It is love* that leads Jesus' disciples to obey His commands just as He obeys His Heavenly Father's commands out of love for Him.[45] The idea of "God in us" represents the most intimate union conceivable between God and men.[46]

God's Grace & Creation Are Hard To Believe

The Gospel/Good News is a message that brings *such good news* that many are afraid that it cannot possibly be true. But, it is true, and it is *never too late* to receive Jesus Christ as one's personal savior and lord. When one makes a conscious heart-felt acknowledgment of repentance of his or her sins and receives Jesus Christ into his or her heart as lord as well as savior, it is known by the Father, who ***immediately reconciles*** that person to Himself as one of His sons with the same inheritance as Jesus Christ. Eventually, when all sin is removed, the children of God will experience a close godly unity that initially was only experienced by the Father, Son, and Holy Spirit.[a] The Father receives ***all*** who follow Jesus as His eternal children ***with all the rights of Jesus, a son***, not as a servant.[b] In fact, Jesus not only calls His followers "brothers" but also His "friends."[c] Being loved as a family member (*agapaō*) and as a friend (*phileō*) produces the highest level of godly love and unity possible.[d]

Are you getting a little nervous because God is calling as many as will receive Him on His terms into His close intimate holy family? Being part of God's intimate eternal loving righteous family places one into a mutually close relationship with the Father. It sounded like heresy to Israel's religious leaders in the first-century when Jesus told them that He was God's son, because by proclaiming to be His Heavenly Father's son, He was proclaiming to be a member of God's immediate family. He had made Himself equal in family membership to the Father.[e]

Does it look like the deeper we dig, the more we have taken away from God's glory by our up-and-coming mature close relationship with Him? The answer is an emphatic "no." In reality, the deeper we look, the more we realize how loving and gracious our Heavenly Father is in working with us even in our sinful and sometimes hostile state. Knowing that we are far from perfect makes it difficult to accept that God's Creation is headed toward a pure sinless love-relationship with Him. But, this is where God's Creation is heading for all who want to be in His holy family and

---

a: (a) John 17:20-23; (b) Gal 4:7; (c) John 15:12-15; (d) Look at John 21:15-17 and others in the Greek; (e) John 5:18.

strive to live out their lives according to His loving righteous way of life.[a] God's planned perfect mutually-interactive relationship within His eternal family leaves *nothing to separate us from Him* in the future when all sin is removed. All of the walls/barriers that sin produces will have been torn down allowing for perfect harmony among all of God's eternal family.

Let's follow Jesus faithfully knowing that God will finish His fantastically good Creation keeping our eyes on Jesus, who is our great eldest brother. With the Father's help and looking to Jesus for leadership, Jesus' followers can have great confidence that in the not-to-distant future, they too will have a very close godly unity with God and one another based on godly love, which produces godly righteousness, grace, and truth within an eternal relationship with God and one another.[b]

a: (a) Rom 5:1-5; 1 John 2:28; (b) Heb 12:1-3; Phil 2:1-16.

6

Becoming a Follower of Jesus Is the Ultimate Victory of Life

And He (Jesus) is the Head of the Body, the Church,
who is the beginning, first out from the dead, that
He may have first place in everything.   Col 1:18[a]

And when all things are subjected to Him, the Son
will subject Himself to Him who subjected all
things with the result that God (the Father) may be
all things in everything.   1 Cor 15:28[b]

Let's keep our mind focused on Jesus and what He teaches. He is the Son of the most High, who out of love and obedience to the Father has rescued us from the ultimate consequence of sin, which is eternal separation from Them, and He teaches us reality.[c] Jesus is worthy to listen to and obediently follow!

In His ministry to us, Jesus taught that *everyone's understanding of our Heavenly Father and His atoning work on everyone's behalf was limited unless they had a desire to do the Father's will.*[d] As you consider our Heavenly Father's love, do you have a genuine desire to please Him? Jesus does. Jesus said that doing the will of His Heavenly Father is what sustained Him even more than food.[e] *Without sin in His life*, Jesus focused on pleasing His Heavenly Father.[f] We should do likewise. If we allow our Heavenly Father to show us our sin, and then we confess

---

a: (a) cf. 1 Cor 12:12-31; (b) cf. 1 Cor 11:3; John 14:28 (c) John 3:14-17; 18:37; cf. 8:31b-32; (d) John 7:17; (e) John 4:34; (f) John 4:34; 8:29.

it before Him, He will cleanse us from all unrighteousness,[a] which in turn helps us more readily return His love and do His will.[47]

It is clear from Scripture that our relationship with our Heavenly Father and Jesus depends on our level of desire to do the Father's will.[b] If we will just turn to God with an open mind and heart reading and responding positively to His Word and leadership,[c] we are able to see more clearly His loving glorious nature. Knowing God more fully normally builds our desire to follow His caring leadership.

If we come to a place where God's goodness and ability help us realize that His way of life is better than anything that we could come up with on our own, we might be willing to relinquish control and submit to the Father's leadership (repentance) and start following Jesus. If anyone comes to that place in his or her life where they trust God enough to want Him to have the final say in their life, He will give that one spiritual birth into His eternal holy family. Immediately he or she becomes a new creation[d] and gladly obeys God out of a growing love and trust for Him and all of His Creation.[e] *Listening to God more than Satan and realizing that the Father and Son are worthy to follow due to a growing love and trust in Them is the ultimate victory placing one into the eternal loving righteous Family of God.*[f]

A Commitment Is Necessary

Have you ever considered the idea that belonging to a certain denomination and/or a certain local church *does **not*** provide you a place with God in Heaven (salvation)? Although there are a fair number of people who subconsciously or

---

a: (a) 1 John 1:9; (b) Matt 12:49b-50; (c) John 8:31b-32; (d) 2 Cor 5:17; (e) 1 John 3:23; 4:7-19; 5:3; (f) John 3:14-17; 6:27-29, 40; 8:12, 51; 10:27-30; 11:25-26; 1 Cor 15:56-57; Eph 1:13-14.

consciously think that their membership in a local church or denomination gives them an automatic place in Heaven with God, in reality, it does not. Being in Heaven with God is purely dependent on being part of His eternal close-knit holy family. *Family members will be with God; non-family members will not.*

As we contemplate Jesus' requirements for those who consider following Him, we come again face-to-face with the reality that God demands that everyone make one critical decision during the physical portion of their eternal life. *In order to be with the Father, Son, Holy Spirit, and the rest of the Saints forever in the New Heaven, each person has to decide prior to death whether or not they will submit to the lordship of a gracious and loving creator, who is our father and worthy of everyone's love and loyalty.* God constantly works among us encouraging all to turn from our self-centered ways to His loving way of eternal life.[a]

Many of us are so caught up in our own self-centered world that we have never given serious consideration to God's perspective on good and evil nor His open invitation to join His eternal intimate holy family. Jesus' parable regarding a kingly invitation to a wedding party applies to all ages because there are always those who are just too busy accomplishing personal ambitions and/or fulfilling personal desires to have time to listen to and accept God's invitation into His eternal holy family.[b] Considering this, Jesus' parable has two important points for everyone:

> (1) do not put off responding in the affirmative to God's invitation into His eternal loving righteous family because there may come a point in your life where you do not hear God's invitation any further; and
> (2) if you accept His invitation to follow Jesus, God is also asking you *to accept the conditions of that invitation*

---

a: (a) Rom 1:18-32; 2:11-16; cf. 2 Peter 3:9; (b) Matt 22:1-14.

(putting on proper clothing) which includes denying self (dying to self), picking up your cross daily, and submitting to His lordship.

Just as in the parable, ***God expects you to act appropriately*** if you accept an invitation into His holy family. If you do not accept the conditions of His invitation, which are clearly stated at multiple places in Scripture such as learning to love, trust, and obey Him, you will end up being separated for eternity from Him and His loving righteous family and sent away to live in the Eternal Lake of Fire, which is often called Hell. ***This breaks God's heart!***

In Jesus' day, when individuals became disciples (students) of a particular teacher, they would normally live in a close relationship with their teacher implementing the teacher's teachings and emulating his way of life. In our modern world, Jesus' followers might be considered ***close apprentices***. Jesus expects His followers (student-disciples) to obey His teachings, emulate His holy way of life, and follow His leadership; His teachings are also His Father's teachings.[a] He even asks His disciples to be willing to lay down their lives for one another.[b] All disciples are expected to give up some things as they follow Him and sometimes suffer according to God's will in order to be part of His great rescue operation.[c]

Following Jesus is not easy, in fact, at times it is difficult and requires hard work, but the rewards are much greater than anything else that we can do as we live out our physical lives. If you are willing and make a genuine commitment to be an active part of God's holy family following Jesus' leadership in this grand rescue operation within the Creation, you will begin to experience excitement and great joy as you join God in helping save those whom you personally have come to love through God.[d] The Holy

---

a: (a) John 8:28; (b) John 13:34; 15:12-13; (c) Phil 1:29-30; Col 1:24-29; cf. Heb 12:1-3; (d) Matt 28:18-20; John 15:1-5.

Spirit will assist and empower you to help others know the Father through Jesus' leadership.[a]

Our growing trust in God is an important part of our development as we follow Jesus. In the eleventh chapter of Hebrews, we are able to gain some insight into the importance of individual faith (trust) in God. As you are read, words such as "belief," "faith," and "trust in the New Testament, keep in mind that these words have all been translated from the same Greek root, *pistis*, depending on context. Greek is the original Mediterranean world language of the New Testament. When viewed from God's perspective, He wants all of us to learn to trust (believe in) Him because He is trustworthy (faithful), able, and keeps His promises. The question for each of us is whether or not we actually have come to know God well enough to realize that He is truly loving, able, and trustworthy.

Although God wants us to get to know Him well enough to step out in faith (trust) and follow Him, many are still distant from God. If you do not feel close to the Father, Son, and Holy Spirit, it would be good to tell God whatever you may be thinking even if you are questioning His existence. If you want to know if God even exists and would like to know Him if He does, make a commitment to read through the Bible asking God to reveal Himself to you. If you really want to know Him and will ultimately try to follow His will; if you do, God will honor that request no matter how distant or none-existent He seems to you at the present.

Hebrews, chapter 11, gives us a list of individuals, who despite their trying circumstances learned to trust God and follow His lead. When the writing of Heb 11 is matched with the accounts recorded in the Old Testament, we note that each of these individuals *grew* in their faith over time. Each one grew to a place of faith–a place of trust in God and His ability–that even when God

---

a: (a) Acts 1:8; Gal 5:22-24.

asked them to do something very difficult, they stepped out in faith and did it:

> (1) consider Noah, who built a very large ship to house hundreds if not thousands of animals on dry ground waiting for a massive world wide flood;[a]
>
> (2) consider Abraham, who was willing to give God back his only biological son after waiting until he was one hundred years old for God to give his son to him;[b]
>
> (3) consider Elijah, who went up on Mount Carmel to confront Baal's false prophets in front of Israel knowing from his faith in God that God would not let him nor Israel down;[c] and
>
> (4) then, consider Jesus, who came into the world that He had created physically living out His life among sinful hostile people, who eventually crucified Him even though He had only done good and spoken truth. He took on the sins of many trusting His Heavenly Father to remove all of His newly acquired sins and raise Him from the dead defeating death for all who listened obediently to Them throughout the entire Creation.[d]

I have witnessed God's goodness and saving work in my own life and many others over the years. One of the biggest obstacle that I have observed for those who have slowed down long enough from their busyness to listen to God is that *they were still enjoying life on the wide-road that leads to destruction too much to submit to Him and His way of life.* Some of these have told me that God has too many rules (commandments) and that they preferred to do things their own way. What this group fails to

---

a: (a) Heb 11:7; (b) Heb 11:17-19; (c) 1 Kings 18:16-39; (d) receive: John 1:12; Rev 3:20; defeating death: John 1:29; Acts 2:22-33; Phil 2:5-11; Rev 11:15; 12:11; 1 John 2:1-2; 3:5.

understand is that God's instructions for life produce the best outcome resulting in the most abundant life. God's commandments are in place to help everyone live caring for one another versus living in a self-centered, selfish environment where people live for themselves many times hurting others along the way.[(a)]

No matter what Satan is doing to deceive people in order to keep them away from God, part of God's Good News (Gospel) for all is that He is patiently working with everyone not wanting any to perish.[(b)] Over time, He gives everyone special spiritual awakening moments to draw those who will listen closer to Him.

Billy Graham tells us in his autobiography, *Just As I Am*, that at just the right time for him, an evangelist, Dr. Mordecai Ham, got through to him as he preached revival services in his area. Billy Graham was spellbound as the Holy Spirit spoke through this evangelist and taught him about Heaven and Hell.[48] *Billy realized through Ham's teaching that he did not have a personal relationship with Jesus and could not depend on his relationship with his parents nor his local church to save him from sin.*[49] After struggling over submission, one night Billy Graham went forward and turned his life over to the rule of God.[50] With that decision to submit his life to God's authority, he came to a place of feeling both peace and joy.[51]

Years later, Billy Graham spoke with George W. Bush, who would become our forty-third president. God used that opportunity to help George Bush realize that although the Bible provided good self-improvement tips, that was not the real message of the Bible. The center of one's life had to shift from self to Jesus, who then becomes lord of one's life.[52] President Bush said that prior to surrendering his life to God, religion had always been part of his life, but he had not been a Believer, a true follower of Jesus.[53]

---

a: (a) Matt 22:36-40; Lev 19:1-3-18-34; (b) 2 Peter 3:9.

Personally, I received God into my life as an eight year old child. At that time, it was God's love that drew me to Him. When I was baptized that same school year at the age of nine in our church-school gymnasium, God gave me a special gift allowing me to feel a little of His great love for *everyone* who was in the gym. That blessing helped me later through some of my own personal trials and helped me become a more caring minister. Although I was saved by God's grace at an early age, He still required me to get to know Him much better as an adult. After going through a very reflective period from age twenty five to twenty eight, I then willingly and gladly submitted to Jesus' leadership as a maturing follower of Jesus. I had come to the place in my life that my understanding of God and His goodness helped me to trust Him enough to turn my life over to Him as an adult knowing that He was always looking out for the best outcome for me and all others. In addition, I started to realize that He was also able to complete the good work that He had started in His Creation including what He was doing in and through me. At twenty eight, I prayed letting God know that I was now ready to follow Jesus without reserve.

Choose Life with God!

Approximately thirty five hundred years ago, God told Israel, a people who had agreed to follow Him, that He had put before them life and good things and death and bad things depending on how they lived. He went on to tell them that if they would return His love, cling to Him (stay close trusting Him), and walk in His ways (obeying His commands, statutes, and judgments), He would bless them in the land that He had given them. They and their descendants would live an abundant life.[a]

---

a: (a) Deut 30:15-19.

Approximately fifteen hundred years later, the Father sent Jesus into our world to teach truth (reality)[a] including the fact that those choosing to live out their lives on the common self-centered road of life would not be entering Heaven.[b] Jesus also explained to all through Thomas that those who wanted to live with God and the others who were holy would need to follow Him and His way of life,[c] which was in reality His Father's way of life.[d]

Our Heavenly Father gives us abundant free will and asks us to *seek* Him for cleansing from past sin and development for the future.[e] In demonstrating His incredible love for us through His Son's *redeeming and reconciling work* on the Cross, our Heavenly Father has given us proof of His sincere desire for a mature loving righteous relationship with each of us. Because of His righteous nature and great love for us, we should willingly subordinate our will to His and allow Him to develop us *into perfectly compatible members* of His holy family. God wants to shape us into His moral image so that we can live together in perfect harmony forever. In his book *Christ's Call to Discipleship*, James Boice reminds us that happiness only comes when we allow God to reorientate our lives to His standards.[54] In order for God to transform our lives, we must die to self and live for Him.

God Will Not Be Mocked

Beware, God will not be mocked![f] If we do not start following Jesus, we will end up being judged according to our decisions and actions during this short physical portion of our eternal lives.[g] Those who listen to God and learn to follow Jesus and His teachings become part of His intimate eternal family.[h]

---

a: (a) John 18:37; (b) Matt 7:13-14; (c) John 14:6; (d) John 8:28;
(e) Matt 6:33; 7:7-8, 14; Luke 11:9-10; cf. Rom 6:22-23; (f) Gal 6:7; cf.
Luke 8:17; 16:15; (g) Rom 2:11-16; 1 Peter 1:17; (h) John 14:21, 23.

Those who do not listen will be judged according to their actions *and* separated from God, His eternal intimate holy family, and all of His Holy Heavenly Host for eternity.[a]

Jesus teaches us that loving God with all our heart, soul, and mind along with loving our neighbors as ourselves fulfills the intent of all of His Father's instructions for proper living.[b] The Hebrew word *Torah* used in the Old Testament literally means "Instruction," which we normally translates into English as "Law." Jesus also stated that He came to fulfill the Instructions of His Father and that nothing of the *Torah* would be removed right up to the time of the finalization of the Creation.[c] Paul taught the Christians of Rome the same thing when he told them that Jesus was the *telos* of the Law, which means that Jesus is the ***fulfillment/completion*** of God's Instructions leading all who are trusting God into righteousness.[d]

Although the *Torah*/Law points out sin and testified to the redeeming work of the coming Messiah,[e] in and of itself, it did not keep anyone from sinning.[f] In fact because of our *corrupted rebellious nature*, God's instructions for an abundant life caused and still causes many to become even more hostile toward Him resulting in more disobedience/sin.[g] Even with this ongoing hostility, God still made eternal life possible through His loving righteous actions.[h] Paul said it this way,

> But, when the fullness of time came, God sent forth His Son, born of a woman, born under the Law in order that those who are under the Law may be redeemed, in order that we may receive sonship. And because *you are sons*, God has sent forth the Spirit from His Son into our hearts crying "Abba, Father."   Gal 4:4-6

---

a: (a) 2 Peter 3:7-10; Rev 20:11-15; (b) Matt 22:37–40; (c) Matt 5:17-19; (d) Rom 10:4; (e) Rom 3:19-20; Gal 3:19, 24; (f) Rom 3:21, 23; 6:23; Gal 3:21; (g) Rom 5:20; (h) Rom 1:16-17.

Through individuals such as Paul, God teaches that He is not partial in His love and guidance, and that He loves everyone more than we can comprehend in our less than perfect condition. Whether or not one has the Written Word of God, when he or she sins, they are responsible for their actions, because the Holy Spirit works in everyone's heart and mind helping everyone know God's desired righteousness. Therefore, only those who follow the *Torah*, the Instructions of God (Law), will be justified (made righteous).[a] The Law was given by God's grace in order to expose sin and lead as many as would listen to Jesus.[b] Does God's grace annul the Law? Paul says emphatically, "*no!*" God's obedient children establish the Law through Jesus atoning death and leadership.[c]

The Good News for those who are being led by the Spirit is that whenever anyone fails to fulfill the Law (sin), Jesus' death on the Cross provides removal of that sin, which allows His true followers to enter into God's presence with a righteousness received from Him.[d]

Turning Off the Wide-road That Leads to Destruction

Jesus taught, "Enter in through the narrow gate because wide is the gate and *spacious/easy is the way* that is leading into destruction, and many are entering in through it because narrow is the gate and *troubling/difficult* is the way that is leading into (eternal) life and few are finding it." Matt 7:13-14

Wow, what a difficult teaching! What makes walking in God's ways so hard compared to living like most people, and why does God make living with Him so difficult if He desires all of His

---

a: (a) Rom 2:11-16; (b) John 1:16-17; Gal 3:19, 24; (c) Rom 3:28-31; cf. 7:12; (d) Rom 8:14-17; 10:1-4; 2 Cor 5:21.

Creation to be part of His eternal holy family? The bottom line is that God wants a freewill family; He does not want a robotic family. He wants everyone to return His pure unbiased love for all,[a] and He wants all to become like Him.

Those who truly seek God and His will for their lives will find the narrow path to eternal life through Jesus. Jesus is the *only* Way to the Father. Indeed, Jesus is the "door" to the Father's presence,[b] and all other so-called paths to God are part of the Broad Path of Destruction, which Satan has so deceptively developed over the years as viable alternatives to God's one and only way of life. The author of Hebrews tells us that Jesus, the true Messiah– the one and only eternal High Priest–offered Himself as an atoning sacrifice, once for all people of all time.[c]

Because God desires a freewill mutually-interactive relationship with all now and forever, He does not force anyone to join Him just as a loving husband would not force nor coerce his bride, who should be a life-long partner, to stay with him. But, God warns us that living a self-centered and selfish life with its corresponding disobedience and sin leads to eternal separation from Him.[d] *We must learn to listen to God and do what He asks of us or our separation will become so complete* that we will feel extreme emotional pain that is hard to comprehend.[e]

Who Do *You* Say That I Am?

After teaching His disciples and having them observe Him and participate with Him in ministering to thousands, Jesus asked them who people thought that He was. The general consensus was that most thought that Jesus was a great prophet.[f] Then Jesus

---

a: (a) 1 John 4:16; (b) John 10:7; 14:6; (c) Heb 4:16-5:10; 10:10-14; cf. 1 Peter 3:18; (d) The second death: Rev 20:14; (e) Luke 13:24-28; (f) Matt 16:14.

asked them, "But you, *what* are you saying that I am [Matt 16:15]?" Simon Peter responded that Jesus was the long awaited Messiah, the Anointed One of God, but he did not stop there. He went on to say that Jesus, the Messiah, was also "the Son of the Living God [Matt 16:16]." These are the most important truths about Jesus that everyone must consider: who and what is Jesus?

Even prior to Jesus' death, God revealed Jesus' identity and upcoming sacrifice to Matthew, who shared this knowledge to the rest of Jesus' disciples. Satan and his demons knew all along the true identity of Jesus as the Messiah (Christ) and Son of God, but they did *not* know about the Father's plan of redemption through His death.[a] *Let's make sure that we who are following Jesus do not let Satan and his helpers keep us so preoccupied with less important things in life,* that we do not help others know the Father, Son, and Holy Spirit and Their great saving love for all.

What I have observed over many years of ministry is that receiving Jesus as lord is very difficult for many. Many come to the point of realizing the validity of Jesus' claim to be the Son of God and savior of the world, but they are still unwilling to submit to His lordship. *Without true submission to the lordship of Jesus Christ, God does not give spiritual birth into His holy family.* Even after understanding this requirement, many do not want to give up some of the things that they are currently doing and submit to Jesus' leadership. For many, it is not that there are major sins in their lives, but that they do not want to take on the responsibility of following Jesus and doing the good works that He might set before them. They like what they are presently doing more than becoming responsible members of God's eternal holy family.

If you are struggling to submit to Jesus' lordship, I want to stress the fact that Satan works hard to keep as many as possible

---

a: (a) Mark 1:34.

from understanding how unbiased and good God is toward all. God asks everyone to seek and know Him and reveals Himself to as many as will obediently listen to Him. As one truly turns his or her life over to Him, God begins a transforming process that develops godly love, faith, joy, and inner peace.[a] In this process, God also liberates His obedient children from sin, which clouds reality and corrupts our closest relationships restricting godly development.[b]

Jesus is the Master Craftsman & Head of the Church

Jesus is the *Master Craftsman* creating all things seen and unseen in Heaven and on Earth. We were created through Jesus for fellowship with Jesus.[c] Jesus following His Father's lead is the Word, the Origin, the Source, from which the Creation came. Jesus existed before all. *He is the eldest*, and it is *through Him* that all things continue. Literally, Jesus has built the universe under His Father's guidance[d] and all that is in it and continually holds it all together.[e] Part of His responsibility as the faithful master craftsman is to lead the Creation.[f] Jesus is the *Head* of the Body, the Church,[g] and sits at the right hand of the Father in power forever.[h]

Jesus Is Teacher and Lord!

Jesus is our *Master Teacher* and *Lord:*

> You (Jesus' disciples) are proclaiming me, "*the* Teacher and *the* Lord," and you are speaking correctly, for I am.   John 13:13[i]

---

a: (a) 1 Cor 13:9-13; Eph 1:18-20; (b) John 8:31b-32, 34-36; (c) Col 1:16; (d) Heb 1:2; (e) Col 1:17; (f) Phil 2:9-11; cf. Heb 1:1-3; (g) Col 1:18; 1 Cor 12; (h) Eph 1:20-21; cf. John 3:31; (i) cf. Luke 6:46.

Jesus is the living Word of God who created everything physically and has given everyone an example of how to live holy lives through His own earthly life and ministry when He perfectly lived out God's Word, the Bible.[a] He only speaks and does what pleases His Father.[b] Today He is still teaching us how to live holy lives through His past examples and ongoing leadership freeing His followers from the bondage of sin, as they follow Him helping as many as possible along the way![c]

Jesus Christ is the Beloved Son

Jesus Christ is the *beloved son* of our Heavenly Father who has redeemed us from our sins. Jesus is the obedient sent son,[d] who is loved very much by the Father and helps us know the Father who cannot be seen with human eyes.[e] Indeed, we can *see the Father's nature* by observing Jesus in all the Father's fulness.[f]

Jesus is Our Loving Eldest Brother

Jesus Christ is also our *loving eldest brother*. He is working in perfect unity with the Father. When considering the normal responsibilities of the oldest son, Jesus is the perfect eldest brother. He is the *first from the dead*, who is the sinless reconciler carrying out His Father's instructions *to reconcile* as many as will listen to His Father.[g] Our Heavenly Father is creating many brothers and sisters for Jesus,[h] who is the sent obedient Son faithfully leading His younger brothers and sisters into the

---

a: (a) John 1:1-3; 8:46; Matt 5:17; summation of God's laws: Matt 22:37-39 (b) John 8:28-29; (c) John 8:31b-32, Matt 28:18-20; (d) John 8:28-29; (e) Col 1:13-14; cf. John 14:7; Heb 1:3; (f) Col 1:19; cf. John 12:45; 14:9; Heb 1:3; (g) Col 1:18-22; cf. Eph 2:13-16; (h) Rom 8:29.

promised perfected New Heaven and New Earth. At that point, Jesus' brothers and sisters will be in their final sinless resurrected state to live with Him, our Heavenly Father, and one another forever in perfect sinless godly unity.[a]

Jesus Is Not Just Another Good Man

Yes, Jesus Christ is *not* just another good man *nor* is He just another great prophet. ***Jesus Christ is the first son of the Living Creator*** who helped His Heavenly Father create this ***temporary world*** in order to create ultimately an enlarged eternal close-knit loving righteous sinless family.[b]

Jesus Provides a Renewed Sinless Life

Jesus is the beginning of renewed resurrected life. He is the ***First out from the Dead.***[c] Our Heavenly Father sent Jesus Christ to die on a cross for all people, and then after His death sentence of three days in Sheol was fulfilled on our behalf, ***He raised Jesus from the dead and set Him over all powers and authorities in Heaven and on Earth.***[d] Today, this same Jesus delivers all who come to trust and obey Him from the destructive plotting of the Evil One, Satan, also known as a devil, who was a murderer and liar from the beginning.[e]

Jesus *is* the sent Son of the one true living God. During Jesus' earthly ministry, many Jewish leaders *ignored* His identity and *rejected* His authority *because of their hardened hearts toward God.* Their hearts had become hardened as they took over

---

a: (a) John 14:6; 20:17; Phil 2:5-8; 3:20-21; cf. John 8:51-58; (b) John 1:3, 10; Heb 1:2; (c) Col 1:18; (d) Eph 1:17-2:10; (e) John 10:10; Rom 10:13; John 8:44.

God's ministry on earth and stopped listening to Him. They would not give up control over their fellow man, which they had wrongfully taken.[a] Therefore, the Father removed all of their responsibility and corresponding authority and transferred it to Jesus' followers, the universal Church.[b] The Temple was destroyed approximately thirty five years after Jesus' resurrection, and Jesus began guiding the Church and will continue doing so through the remaining years of the Creation.

Throughout the centuries following Jesus' earthly ministry, many have continued to *ignore* His identity and *reject* His authority because of hardened hearts. Those who hear and receive Jesus Christ hear and receive the Father. Those who hear and receive Jesus' disciples hear and receive Jesus.[c] The Father has and is speaking to all who listen through Jesus, and presently Jesus is speaking to all who listen through the Holy Spirit, Scripture, and His followers, who make up His Body and the (universal) Church.

If you are convinced that Jesus is the Son of God but have not submitted to His lordship, pray that God will show you His heart and worthiness as you read further. If you pray for God's guidance, He will reveal Himself to you. You will come to see that He is worthy of your love and obedience, and from there God will encourage you to solidify a genuine commitment to follow Jesus wherever He leads.

Jesus Alone Provides Access to the Father

When Jesus said that He is the Way, the Truth, and the Life, and that no one is able to appear before the Father except through Him,[d] the Sent Son was making it perfectly clear that

---

a: (a) Matt 21:33-39; (b) Matt 21:43; (c) Matt 10:40; (d) John 14:6.

eternal life with the Father only occurs for those *who are in close association with Him*. In one of His sermons on a mountain, the apostle Matthew tells us that Jesus stated emphatically that on the Day of Judgment there will be many who will say that they had called Him "lord" and had done many things in His name. Yet, in reality, they had never really started obediently listening to His Father nor following Him. For those individuals, Jesus will declare, "I have never known you; depart from me you who have been working contrary to the Law [Matt 7:21-23; 12:50]."[a]

The apostle John not only remembered Jesus saying that He was the *only way* to God, but he also remembered Jesus using the metaphorical image of being *the one and only "door"* declaring that He was the only point of access to the Father.[b] Jesus taught His disciples that those seeking a personal relationship with our Heavenly Father must come through Him:

> *I am the door!* It is through me that if someone enters, he shall be saved—indeed he shall come and go and find pasture.   John 10:9

Jesus taught that the way to God was through returning God's love, which led to *obedience*. If one follows the normal course of building their own security without paying attention to God, they are in reality still following the broad road that leads to eternal shame, unrest, and suffering. Obedience to Jesus' leading is the one and only path that leads to eternal life with God, because Jesus is *the only "gate," the only "door,"* leading into the Kingdom of Heaven.[c] Our Heavenly Father confirms this same truth through the apostle Paul, who taught that Gentile Believers had the same access to the Father as their Jewish brothers and

---

a: (a) cf. Rom 2:11-16; (b) John 10:17; (c) Matt 7:13-14; Luke 13:24; John 10:7.

sisters who were following Jesus because Jesus was their common access through His redeeming work on the Cross.[a]

Our Heavenly Father is worthy of our submission and loyalty and so is Jesus.[b] If we did not receive Jesus into our lives as children, submission to Him as an adult may be the most difficult act of the will for many. As an adult, it is harder to give up personal sovereignty and replace it with God's lordship until one realizes how much God loves everyone and how able He really is to bring those who listen to Him into the perfected New Heaven and New Earth where sin and its earlier corruption will no longer occur.[c] So what is God asking of us during this present physical part of our eternal life journeys?

Denying Self

The first point that Jesus made for all who were interested in following Him is that they must allow God to lead and in so doing must die to self,[d] which means that they must lay aside some or all of their personal ambitions and follow Jesus. This does not mean that God wants everyone to be a full-time minister, but it does mean that *all of Christ's followers will minister on some level* and that all who follow Jesus will live out their lives under Jesus' lordship and not their own. In his book *Christ's Call to Discipleship*, James Boice stated that earlier followers of Jesus would never understand how people today profess to follow Jesus and ignore self-denial, which is the very essence of being one of Jesus' followers, His disciples.[55]

Those who follow Jesus will not be working out success according to the world's standards but instead according to God's

---

a: (a) Eph 2:18; (b) Rev 4:11; 5:8-10; (c) Rom 8:18-23; (d) John 12:24-26; cf. Luke 14:26.

leadership. God asks all of Jesus' followers to give of their resources, which include talent, time, and economic resources. The good news for those who make a genuine commitment to follow Jesus is that when they become part of God's eternal holy family, they also become part owner of everything. Although it is not apparent presently, in reality not only do Jesus' followers share in His glory, but they are also fellow heirs with Him and one another.[a]

Keep in mind that what we own with God is nothing compared to our developing loving kind relationship with God and other Saints, which brings great inner peace and joy. What we give up in personal success and possible material possessions during this present age to serve God, we gain back more than our minds can possibly imagine both in this present world and in Heaven. In reality, when one turns away from a self-centered life to God's way of life, joy and inner peace begin to grow as they follow Jesus.

Worldly Pleasures & Personal Ambitions

In a kind of seductive and deceptive way, Satan deceives many into believing that if they start listening to God, they will have to give up much more than they will receive. Many people fail to follow Jesus when they are young for this very reason. I have personally known some who came to understand God's love in some limited way, but failed to grasp the severity of the consequences of not following God's leading and ways for their lives. Just as the Laodiceans with their material wealth, they did not realize how much God would improve their present quality of life, if they would just turn to Him.[b]

---

a: (a) John 20:17; Rom 8:17, 28-30; (b) Rev 3:15-18; cf. Rom 6:22.

Most of us know that God is asking us to follow His lead and give up some of our personal time and resources in order to help others physically and spiritually, but we do not want to do so. The concept of helping others beyond our own immediate family is foreign to much of the world. The idea of denying self makes no sense to those who do not trust a loving Creator to look out for their best interests.

Jesus taught that those who desire to follow Him must start by "denying" themselves. They must let go of their personal desires common to this world including worldly success and obediently follow Him as the Father helps them grow in their love for all.[a] For many, Jesus was and still is asking too much. It is amazing how much time can be wasted on being entertained, entertaining, engaging in sports, social networking, doing hobbies, using technology, or just spending extra time with family or friends at the expense of becoming involved with God and others. These things are fine in proper moderation, but never good when they become all consuming whether separately or collectively.

In reality, it is all about willingness. Over time, I have seen some who initially would not follow Jesus eventually start following Him and consequently learn to care more about others. As people learn to care about others, they also learn that it brings more joy to give than to receive. *When people finally begin to realize that God gives much more than He asks of anyone, it becomes easier to give up control and follow Jesus.*

Considering an extreme case, there was an individual, Bill, whom I had witnessed to many times in the past who did not receive Jesus as lord and savior until the end of his life. After working within our company for several years, Bill eventually left for another job. After not hearing from nor seeing Bill for ten to fifteen years, he called me from a hospital. He told me that he was

---

a: (a) 1 John 2:15-17; 3:23.

dying from a liver ailment brought about by too much drinking. So, I went to meet with Him in his hospital room knowing through the Holy Spirit's leading that he had never started following Jesus. We spoke for a couple hours, and he finally realized–at the end of his life–that it would be an honor and privilege to start following Jesus.

He repented and asked God's forgiveness because of his worldly lifestyle and committed to follow Jesus Christ for the rest of his life knowing that God probably would not heal him physically. God did not heal him physically but immediately healed him spiritually and gave him a sense of love, peace, and joy that was supernatural and stayed with him for the rest of his physical life. Over the next three months, I visited him on a regular basis and knew that his organs were slowly shutting down. As I watched his final decline, he noticed that I was feeling sad about his physical state, and he told me not to be sad because he was the happiest he had ever been in his life. He had become a child of God, and starting with his own family, he told people about the importance of following Jesus (witnessing) until he died. Through Bill's changed life, I was reminded again of God' grace and the truth of Scripture, which said that *those who receive the living water of God will never thirst again and that the Living Water residing in them, the Holy Spirit, would become a living spring, a source of life, for others.*[a]

Repentance: the Final Frontier

The idea of repentance is translated from various forms of the Old Testament Hebrew words *shuv* and *naham* and the New Testament Greek words *epistrephō* and *metanoeō*. Within biblical

---

a: (a) John 4:14 and 7:38-39.

meaning, it indicates a change of heart, a change of one's life and lifestyle, *and* a turning from self and sin to God and His righteous way of life. *It is a change of the heart that triggers action.* There is a true commitment to stop living for self and start living for God and others. In reality, God knows everyone's heart and true repentance brings about conversion, being spiritually born into God's holy family, which is the work of God and God alone.[a] We learn from Scripture that repentance is the last hurdle to overcome. It is the last frontier as individuals come to the place of asking God for forgiveness of sins *and turn* from their personal self-centered lifestyles to Him and His way of caring life for all. *Repentance is necessary for all who wish to become part of God's eternal holy family!*[b]

In 2 Chron 30:9 and Neh 1:9, it is written that if Israel "turned back" to God after serving other gods and being expelled from their land, God would give them grace through their captors and allow them to return to their land. In Jer 18:8, God said that if *any nation* turned away from doing wickedness, He would relent of their up-coming judgment. God's response to repentance, *individually and corporately*, has always been the same. If an individual repents or God's people as a whole repent within nations, God will make individuals and/or nations whole.

In Acts 15:3, the Greek noun *epistrophē* is presently translated as "conversion" by many, but note that it would have been better translated as the "turning" of the Gentiles (toward God). Luke used this word to describe a change of lordship and lifestyle for those Gentiles who had given up their pagan lifestyles to follow Jesus. In addition, we see Luke using various verb forms of this noun to describe a "turning" to God by both Jew and Gentile. In Luke 1:16, we see a prophecy given about Jesus, the Christ (Messiah): He will *turn* many of the Sons of Israel *back* to

---

a: (a) John 1:12-13; (b) Matt 3:2; 4:17; Acts 2:38; 20:21.

the Lord, their God. In Acts 11:21, Luke speaks of a connection between believing (trusting) and "turning to" the Lord Jesus. In Acts 14:15, he reports that Paul proclaimed the Good News to all in Lystra in order "to turn them away" from empty-vain things and "turn them to" the Living God.

In Acts 26:19-20, Luke speaks of repentance being part of the process of "turning to" God. He recalled Paul telling King Agrippa that he, Paul, had been obedient to God's revelation to him, and therefore, he was proclaiming the Good News to many including the Gentiles telling them "to repent and turn to the (one true) God" *doing works worthy of repentance.*

God speaks to all people of all ages about good and evil.[a] *Biblical conversion occurs through God's action after one "turns to Him" giving up their own way of life and submitting to Him and His ways.* When someone willingly repents turning from a self-centered posture to God and His way of life, a genuine conversion, a spiritual birth into God's holy family occurs.[b]

When one listens to God and starts to follow Him based on a developing love for Him, trust in God grows through *experiencing* His trustworthiness.[c] All who commit to follow God and His way of life experience a fuller and fuller life here-and-now as God shapes their lives making them more and more righteous, and He will finish their perfection upon physical death.[d] Then eventually, all of God's children will be completed in their final form when they receive their resurrected bodies.[e] All who have learned to trust and obey God over the ages become part of His close-knit loving righteous (holy) family and kingdom forever.

As we learn about God and His desire for us to join Him forever, what might hinder us from submitting to His lordship and receiving Him into our lives? When looking at biblical repentance,

---

a: (a) Rom 1:18-2:16; (b) 1 John 2:17; (c) Gal 5:6; Heb 5:14; cf.
2 Peter 1:1-11; (d) Rom 6:22; 1 John 3:1-2; (e) Phil 3:20-21.

the key to "turning" to God is *His love*.[a] There are quite a few who might respond positively to God's love,[b] if they would just slow down and listen to Him above all of the competing voices–of which many are satanic distractions. When one turns to God, repentance is manifested through a developing trust and obedience toward Him.[c] God's people learn through Jesus' leadership to do more and more for others as He continues to develop godly love in their hearts. Keep in mind that godly love does no harm.[d]

The New Testament is clear regarding the spiritual impact of turning to God. One must receive God and turn from self to Him and His way of life in order for God to give that one spiritual birth into His holy family. And many, like the Prodigal Son, have to experience some difficult event or series of events before they will slow down and allow God to help them come to their senses. There are others to whom God is able to speak during quiet moments. Keep in mind that God is creating His eternal intimate holy family, and if He can awaken someone spiritually, He will reveal Himself and His way of life to that one at the appropriate times.

Carrying One's Cross & Experiencing Jesus' Joy

As Christ's followers learn to put personal ambitions aside, God asks each to carry their own personal crosses willingly suffering on behalf of others. This is not easy, but worthwhile eventually producing great joy. Kyle Idleman, a pastor of one of the largest churches in the US, came to the point of realizing that he had been trying to bring people to God through messages that were appealing, comfortable, and convenient.[56] Then, he came to the realization that *Jesus did no such thing*. Jesus emphasized repentance, surrender, and brokenness more than forgiveness,

---

a: (a) 1 John 4:16; (b) 1 John 4:19; (c) Gal 5:6; John 14:21, 23; (d) 1 Cor 13:4-8; Gal 5:13.

salvation, and happiness.[57] Jesus taught that His followers were to deny self, pick up their crosses daily, and follow Him.[a] Idleman realized that a cross best expressed Jesus' life and ministry and His invitation for others to join Him in humility, suffering, and death.[58]

Although Jesus was eternal like His Father and had physically created the universe and all that is physically in it, He did not think it beneath Him to humble Himself and die for His Creation giving life to all who obediently respond. *Jesus is an example of godly love in action!*[b] Jesus' ministry did not stop with His death and resurrection but is still ongoing from His place in Heaven at the right hand of the Father as He leads the Church.[c]

God does not tell us in advance what each of our individual crosses on behalf of others will be, yet He has specific duties for each to help bring His Creation to completion.[d] There are no surprises for God. He knows what He is doing and how we will respond. He asks that *we make a commitment to follow Him* based on His character and ability. He tells all who follow Jesus that they *will suffer, but they will also experience great joy* as they join Him in rescuing people from present self induced hurt and future pain and suffering.[e] Each of us must ask ourselves if we are willing to give up some or all of our personal aspirations as we begin to learn to trust Him with our physical and spiritual lives.

Sometimes, we make half-hearted commitments that end up leaving us without fulfillment due to our lack of faith. God is looking for genuine trust because of *His faithful character and great ability.* He is looking for true commitment, sacrifice, and allegiance in the face of whatever circumstances that He allows in our lives. In all cases for those following God and His ways, *He uses His people out of every tribe and nation to represent Him to the world. Those who follow Him are His priests and light for all*

---

a: (a) Luke 9:23; (b) Phil 2:5-8; (c) Eph 1:20-23; (d) Eph 2:10; Phil 2:13; (e) example: Paul- Col 1:24.

people.[a] Those who follow Jesus are His ambassadors to the rest of the world.[b]

After God showed His love to Israel and rescued them from slavery in Egypt, the whole nation agreed to follow Him not fully understanding His holiness nor priestly demands.[c] Many had not made a long-term commitment and thus continued to sin and rebel against Him. The vast majority of the adult generation that God led out of Egypt did not make it into the promised land because they would not allow Him to help them mature through the trials that He set before them.[d] Except for two individuals, Joshua and Caleb, the older generation never experienced the better way of life that God has for those of every generation who learn to follow His lead out of a growing love for Him and His ways.

A New Creation

If we continue to take time to *study* and *act* on God's Word, Jesus Christ and our Heavenly Father teach us to know the reality of both the physical and spiritual world in which we live. As we obey God, He matures us allowing us to live in a closer relationship with Him. Our character will eventually become totally transformed to be like Jesus' resulting in a very close mature relationship after our physical death or resurrection experience.[e] But even prior to physical death, Jesus' followers immediately start experiencing transformation:

> (1) they immediately *become new creations* "in Christ" through spiritual birth into God's eternal close-knit holy family;[f]
> (2) they immediately *start experiencing the sanctifying work of the Holy Spirit;*[g] those who have been born of God

---

a: (a) Matt 5:14-16; 1 Peter 2:9-10; (b) 2 Cor 5:20; (c) Ex 19:4-6;
(d) Num 14:20-35; (e) 1 Thess 4:13-17; (f) 2 Cor 5:17; Eph 1:13-14;
(g) Rom 6:22.

sin less and less and less over time due to God's guidance, which is made known through the Holy Spirit living in them;[a]

(3) they are *immediately justified* before God although their justification is not realized until they meet God face-to-face.[b] In reality, with spiritual birth into God's holy family comes the miracle through which God removes their sins (unrighteous actions) and they become Jesus' unrighteous actions on the Cross, and they are made righteous before Him through His righteousness;[c] and

(4) as they follow Jesus, they are *empowered by the Holy Spirit and **tell others about God's goodness.**[d]

Experiencing Jesus' Joy

What did it cost God to perfect those who learn to trust Him over the ages? From Scripture, we find that *it was necessary for Jesus' atoning death to provide sin removal* from those who want to come into God's eternal presence.[e] Sin cannot be just covered over with a bandage. The wound has to be totally healed to the point that there is no trace that a wound ever existed. The Psalmist David once said that due to God's loving-kindness, He has removed the transgressions of those who love and respect Him as far as the East is separated from the West.[f]

---

a: (a) 1 John 3:9; (b) Rom 5:1; 1 John 3:2; (c) Rom 1:16-17; 2 Cor 5:21; 1 Peter 2:24; (d) Rom 8:14; Acts 1:8; (e) John 3:14-15; (f) Ps 103:11-12.

So how did God remove our sins from us allowing us to be with Him for eternity? Paul uses three basic thoughts to express how God removes all sin from those who learn to trust and obey Him out of a growing love:

(1) in Galatians 3:13-14, Paul stated that Jesus, the Messiah, became a *curse* for those who are trusting in God so that those who are "in Christ" might receive the blessings of Abraham. From the Old Testament, it is clear that when someone violates God's laws, he or she is cursed in the sense that judgment for sin is coming. The penalty for sin (doing wrong) is separation from God and His community (spiritual death). Jesus, the Messiah, became a curse on our behalf, was judged guilty, crucified on our behalf, and spent three days—which might have been like 3000 years[a]—in Sheol (spiritual jail) separated from our Heavenly Father on our behalf;

(2) in Colossians 2:13-14, Paul stated that when we were dead (separated from God) because of our transgressions, Jesus' atoning work on the Cross allowed God to take the master list with each of our names and corresponding criminal charges against us and ***nail it to Jesus' cross condemning Him and cancelling out the charges against us;*** and

(3) Paul explicitly stated in 2 Corinthians 5:21 that when Jesus Christ died on a cross on our behalf, ***the Father transferred our sin to Him,*** who had been sinless up to that moment. Jesus took on all of the sins of those who learned to return God's love, and God's righteousness was transferred to them. In 1 Peter 2:21-24, Peter helps us understand the same thing.

---

a: (a) 2 Peter 3:8.

Within 2 Corinthians 5:21, we learn that our sins have been replaced with God's righteousness so that we will stand before Him one hundred percent righteous. *This is a miracle of gigantic proportion*.

It is easy to consider God's saving miracle on our behalf, thank Him for dying in our place, and go on with life as usual. But, this is where we need to really *pause and consider* what God has done for us, and what He wants in return. *At great cost to Himself through suffering, pain, and death, God took on the sins of all who learn to trust Him*. In exchange, our Heavenly Father asks everyone to learn to trust Him and Jesus enough to follow Jesus.

Jesus knew that dying physically on a cross and dying spiritually (separation from His Heavenly Father) was going to produce *terrible pain and suffering* both physically and emotionally. Just before He was arrested to go to His death on a cross, He asked the Father one last time if there was another way to take care of our sin, but in reality, He already knew that His atoning death was the only way; it was necessary.

It is hard to imagine what the Father went through emotionally when He saw His Son being rejected by His own people.[a] Think of the emotional pain of both the Father and Son when the very people whom Jesus had ministered to for three years doing only good turned against Him and asked for Barabbas, a known criminal, to be set free instead of the loving righteous Jesus.[b] Imagine the Father's emotional pain when Jesus was humiliated, scourged, and died physically a cruel and painful physical death on a cross. Then imagine the most painful part of all: because Jesus took on the sins of those who learn to trust God, the Father had to turn His back on His obedient faithful Son who then become a sinner. Consider Jesus' abandonment by the Father when our sins were placed on Him. As Jesus was dying, He cried

---

a: (a) John 1:11; (b) John 18:39-40.

out loudly, "My God, my God, for what reason have you abandoned me [Matt 27:46]?" Jesus knew why His Heavenly Father had just abandoned Him: He had become a sinner. That proclamation was to remind us of the great cost that He and the Father were paying for our redemption.

We know from Jesus' discussion with one of the thieves that He had forgiven him and that particular thief would be in upper Sheol (Paradise) with Him that very day,[a] and we know from multiple places in Scripture that Jesus would be in Sheol (Hades) for three days preaching the Good News of how God the Father and He had arranged to eradicate sin.[b] After spending three days in Sheol on our behalf, our Heavenly Father raised Him from the dead,[c] and cleansed Him from all the sin that He had taken on through His death on a cross.[d]

Those who were trusting God prior to the Cross were finally able to be made perfectly righteous through His death allowing them to be in God's immediate presence after Jesus finished His atoning work. Jesus' death on humanity's behalf removes all sin from all who submit to the loving Creator for all time. ***The major spiritual battle that was critical for a saving opportunity for all mankind had now been won.***[e] This battle was won through Jesus' obedient and sacrificial life and death.

This same Jesus who willingly endured the shame and suffering of death on a cross as a criminal on our behalf ***simultaneously experienced great joy*** because He was providing salvation for all who desire a righteous life with God.[f] ***This is godly love! What are you willing to do for your friends?***

If we consider both the ***suffering*** *and* ***joy*** of Jesus, we will start to understand the heart and mind of God, which is also becoming the heart and mind of Jesus' followers.[g] Jesus'

---

a: (a) Luke 23:43; (b) Isa 53; 1 Peter 2:24; cf. Gal 3:8-21; (c) Acts 2:31; cf. Eph 4:7-12; (d) 1 John 2:1; (e) John 19:30; 1 Cor 15: 50-58; Rev 5:9-10; 11:15; (f) John 15:10-11; 17:13; Heb 12:2; (g) 1 Cor 2:16.

followers are learning to love as God loves and thereby experience godly joy and excitement as they minister to those around them and introduce them to the Father, Son, Holy Spirit, and Christ's Body, the universal Church.[a]

God Requires a Personal Decision

Jesus said that *if we are not willing to deny ourselves and carry our individual assigned crosses and follow Him, we are <u>not able</u> to be His disciples.*[b] So, is God worthy of our turning from self to Him? *Of course He is worthy!* If you do not feel a sense of awe and reverence toward God, you are still too focused on yourself. When we come to realize what God has done for each of us, the proper response would be to return God's love by receiving Him into our lives.

Think of it this way. If you have not yet come to understand *why you should joyfully follow Jesus and stop looking for personal gain*, you are still being deceived by Satan. If you have any real understanding on what is spiritually going on around you, you would want to do your part in building God's eternal close-knit holy family. Consider this: what would you personally be willing to do to save someone whom you love dearly from a terrible fate such as dying in a fire, drowning, or pulling them out of the rubble of a bad auto accident? Most of us would do whatever it takes including possibly giving our own lives to save those whom we love dearly.

Rescuing others from an eternal state of shame, unrest, and ongoing pain and helping them to improve their lives right now is what God is asking of us as we join Him in doing the good works that He has assigned to each of us.[c] Jesus gave His life that we

---

a: (a) Acts 13:52; 15:3; 1 John 1:4; (b) Luke 14:26-27; cf. Matt 10:38; (c) Eph 2:10.

may live a better life now and forever.[a] *Jesus is asking us to follow Him in joy and suffering* as we pick up our individual crosses and suffer for others because of what He has done for us *and* because our love is growing for all.[b] *If we have not yet allowed God to teach us to truly care about those around us, we probably will not be willing to suffer on their behalf.*[c]

Consider what Paul said about his own suffering for others. In a letter to the Saints living at Colossae, Paul said,

> Now, I am *rejoicing* in those things suffered on your behalf and I am supplying the needs of the afflictions of Christ in my body on behalf of His Body, which is the Church, of which I have become a minister according to my stewardship (overseeing) from God, ...   Col 1:24-25

Paul wanted Jesus' followers at Colossae to understand that his suffering was not something that destroyed his joy but instead enhanced it due to the advancement of the Gospel, which brought many out of the bondage of darkness into God's Kingdom.[d] Paul was following Jesus and was being empowered by Him to present as many as possible before God at the Judgment Day *complete* in Jesus Christ.[e]

In a similar way, Paul told the Corinthians that they were sharing in Jesus' followers' ongoing afflictions due to spiritual warfare with Satan as they proclaimed the Gospel.[f] He went on to tell the Saints residing at Corinth that the Macedonian Saints, who were also being afflicted for their trust in God as they followed Jesus, were experiencing great joy through their generous behavior

---

a: (a) John 10:10-11; 1 John 3:16; (b) John 15:20; cf. Matt 10:25; (c) 1 John 3:17; 4:11-16; (d) Col 1:13-14; (e) Col 2:28-29; (f) 2 Cor 1:3-11; 4:7-10.

towards others.[a] Paul also encouraged the Thessalonians to continue to do God's work in spite of the afflictions that they were suffering as they followed Jesus. Paul and his fellow co-laborers were rejoicing because the Saints at Thessalonica were continuing to grow in their faith.[b]

Following Jesus Is an Ongoing Relationship

Jesus said, "Behold, I am standing at the door (of each person's life) and knocking. If anyone hears my sound (from knocking) and opens the door, I shall come in onto Him and I will fellowship with him and he with Me."   Rev 3:20

Jesus is our perfect example and leader. Jesus takes pleasure in doing and saying those things that His Heavenly Father desires.[c] Like the Father, Jesus loves all people dearly. *Jesus came to serve, not to be served.*[d] He consistently spent His time and energy teaching as He healed the sick and cast out demons. His main command was to "repent;" "go and sin no more."[e] There were many nights that Jesus just dropped where He had been ministering without a comfortable place to sleep.[f] There were many times when He could have used some rest but pushed on bringing light to as many as possible during His short ministry on earth. All of this culminated with many asking for His death and the release of a known criminal.[g] Jesus does not ask for anyone's sympathy, but He does ask for our love and obedient service to others in response to His obedient service and suffering for all.[h]

---

a: (a) 2 Cor 8:1-4; (b) 1 Thess 2:14-3:13; (c) John 4:34; 8:26-29;
(d) Matt 20:28; Mark 10:45; (e) Matt 4:17; 11:20-24; John 5:14; 8:11;
cf. Matt 3:2; (f) Matt 8:20; Luke 9:58; (g) Matt 27:11-22; Mark 15:6-
13; Luke 14:13-21; John 18:37-19:16; (h) John 15:10.

Although many start out wanting a savior but not a lord, every individual must eventually choose whether he or she wishes to follow God and His caring way of life or follow the current leader of chaos and bad choices, Satan, with his destructive ways.[a] *As some start listening to God and realize how good He actually is, and that He only wants the best for each person, some come to a place in their lives where they trust God enough to turn their lives over to Him wanting to experience His goodness more fully. This results in a life altering change where they joyfully receive Him as both lord and savior.* When that happens, God begets them spiritually into His holy family and starts His faithful work of molding and shaping them into His image.[b] In the Bible, this godly maturing process of becoming holy is called "sanctification." Depending on context and grammar, the words "holy" and "sanctification" are translated from the Hebrew root *qadosh* (Old Testament) and the Greek root *hagios* (New Testament). The primary idea behind these words is that one is living a life that is *set apart* from the ways of this world, *dedicated* to God, and *emulating* God's loving righteous lifestyle.

Jesus has no room for lukewarm followers.[c] When individuals truly follow Jesus, their actions and words become more and more like His, and Jesus helps them to follow His lead instead of Satan's. If one continues to follow Satan knowingly or unknowingly, he or she stays on that wide easy road (life path) that eventually leads to eternal separation from God.[d]

What Do You Say?

From what you have already read, you know that you have been created by God to be part of His eternal loving

---

a: (a) John 3:36; 8:43-46; 14:23; 1 John 3:7-10; cf. Deut 30:15-16; and others; (b) John 3:16; Eph 1:13-14; Rom 6:22; 10:9; (c) Rev 3:16; (d) 1 John 3:7-11; 5:19-21.

righteous family. This is your primary purpose for existence! God wants you voluntarily to join Him and the rest of His holy family. When you willingly turn your life over to Him for justification and development, God works in your life shaping your character to become more and more like Jesus'. Whether you die physically or are taken up to God without dying (rapture),[a] God completes His work in His obedient children,[b] and when you stand before Him entering your assigned place in eternity within His holy family, you will be morally like Jesus standing before God clothed in your good works and His righteousness without any sin.[c]

God asks all to respond positively to His great love through repentance, obedience to His Written Inspired Word, and obedience to the leading of His Son through the help of the Holy Spirit. Prior to making a commitment to follow Jesus, no one can purify themselves enough to be presentable in his or her own righteousness,[d] but the good news is that *God receives you just as you are.* If we have a desire to do God's will and come to Him committed to follow Jesus as our lord and savior, *it is God who cleanses us of our sins.*[e] As we start a committed life with God, we learn to trust and obey Him more as His great love for all is understood more fully.

At this point in your life, if you have not already become a follower of Jesus, it is my prayer that you now are willing to repent (turn from your way of life to follow God's way of life) and talk (pray) to the Father asking for forgiveness for all past wrongdoing and asking Jesus to become your personal *lord* as well as *savior.*

---

a: (a) 1 Thess 4:13-18; Rev 20:4-6; (b) Rom 8:28-30; 1 John 3:1-2; (c) 2 Cor 5:21; (d) Rom 3:23; (e) 1 John 1:9; cf. 2 Cor 5:21; Col 2:13-14; 1 Peter 2:24.

Let's Talk Commitment

What do you know?

(1) Do you know that Jesus Christ, the Savior of the World, was sent out of Heaven from our Heavenly Father as a human (incarnate) like you and I, lived a sinless life exemplifying His Father's Word, died on a cross for the removal of potentially everyone's sin, was buried, and was raised from the dead three days later according to Scripture?;[a]

(2) do you know that sin causes disharmony, hurt, corruption, and destruction and needs to be removed from your life in order that you may be reconciled to the Father, Son, Holy Spirit, and the rest of God's holy family?;[b] and

(3) do you know that you personally need to confess your sins and ask God into your life as lord and savior, and then He provides eternal sin removal (justification)?[c]

Many people go to church, read their Bibles, go to Bible studies, make good plans to follow Jesus, but never make a solid commitment to follow Him. *Many in our churches today have never actually stepped out in faith and started following Jesus.* If you would like to be part of God's eternal holy family and have not done so yet, this is what is required: *commit to follow Jesus, step out in faith, and start following!* What God said to His people through His prophet Malachi about trust and obedience regarding the tithe is applicable to everyone's life in all things: *test God!* Step out in faith (trust) as the Holy Spirit leads and see how God will bless you as He works with you.[d]

---

a: (a) John 1:29; 3:14-17; Luke 1:26-35; 1 Cor 15:4; (b) Rom 8:18-23; cf. 3:23 & 6:23; Eph 2:11-22; 2 Cor 5:17-21; (c) 1 John 1:8-10; Rom 10:9; Gal 3:13-14; Col 2:13-14; 2 Cor 5:21; 1 Peter 2:24; (d) Mal 3:10.

Considering God's pure nature of love, which has been demonstrated by His actions for all and shown by His words as recorded in Scripture, have you come to a place where you trust Him enough to submit your life to His leadership?[a] Once you have turned to God and have submitted to His lordship,[b] He will never lose nor forsake you.[c]

Jesus asks all who are considering submission to His leadership to consider what He is asking prior to submitting.[d] He tells all who wish to be part of God's holy family that if they are not willing to join Him in building His Father's eternal holy family, the Father will not allow them to be part of His family.[e] Jesus' marching orders for all family members have one common point, "As you are going (living your lives), *make disciples!* [Matt 28:19]" Without being willing to follow God's leadership in helping to reconcile a lost world unto Himself,[f] individuals will not be empowered by the Holy Spirit, which *enables* them to be disciples of Jesus.[g]

As we presently come to a place of commitment, I am reminded that we all need Jesus as both lord and savior in every aspect of our lives. I know that God will lead all who listen to Him out of an unfulfilled life into one filled with love, inner peace, joy, excitement, and great expectation. In addition, I know that as individuals start listening to God, their lives change for the better *immediately* and *forever.*[h] There is no greater blessing for a parent or spouse than for a loved one to start following Jesus.

Ok, *now* is the time. If you have *not* already turned to God, you should do so now. *It's time to make a commitment to follow Jesus.* **Making a commitment to follow Jesus is the ultimate victory of God's Creation!** Remember that Jesus does not accept lukewarm followers. With a firm commitment to follow Jesus, *God*

---

a: (a) 1 John 4:16; cf. 1:3; Rom 10:9-13; (b) repentance- 2 Peter 3:9; (c) John 10:9-17, 27-30; (d) Luke 14:26-33; (e) John 15:1-2, 8; (f) Matt 7:21; cf. John 7:17; (g) Luke 14:27, 33; Acts 1:7-8; (h) Rom 6:22.

will come immediately into your life through the eternal indwelling of the Holy Spirit and start developing and empowering you so that you are able to live out your life in godly love and bless many. If you try to wait until you become righteous enough to approach God, you will physically die first. Everyone needs God's help in becoming righteous. *So let's pray to God asking forgiveness of our wrongdoing and committing to follow Jesus.* Pray this prayer or anything similar to it to our Heavenly Father, who knows your heart, *and trust Him to start His redemptive and transforming work in you immediately:*

> Heavenly Father, thank you for sending your Son, Jesus Christ, who put the universe together, to die on everyone's behalf. I know that you love me beyond my comprehension. Through Jesus' atoning death, you have provided the one and only way to remove all my sin and replace it with your righteousness. I ask for your forgiveness of my sins. I know that sin has kept me from having a close personal relationship with you, and that by submitting to your loving righteous leadership, you will help me become a caring righteous member of your eternal holy family. Please help me to walk in your loving righteous ways and follow your leading. It is my pleasure to follow Jesus Christ faithfully now and forever. I trust you to help me walk in your ways and ultimately bring me into your eternal presence. Father, thank you for creating me and patiently waiting for me to receive you into my life. You are worthy to praise and follow! I pray that from now on, my life will bring honor and glory to you as people see my life becoming more and more like Jesus'.   Amen.

Being Liberated by God

OK, *now you have done it!* If you have prayed that prayer or one similar to it now or in the past, the angels in Heaven celebrated with God over your decision to follow Jesus.[a] God starts your reconciled life with Him by saying to the rest of the Church, *"loose (unbind) him and let him go his way* [John 11:43-44].*"* Just as Lazarus needed to be loosed from his burial wrappings, each of Christ's new followers need help from God and His Church to remove the wrappings of this world that bind them from godly living.

God expects you to connect–if you are not already connected–to a local church, and He expects the members of that church to have a genuine interest in freeing you from your worldly thinking and actions through proper assimilation of His Word, which comes from continual prayer, sound study, proper application of His Word, and a submissive heart to His teaching and leading.

Now that you have turned from your sins and current way of life to follow Jesus (repentance), *life is going to become new and exciting.* You are now a new creation: you are officially a child of God, a king and priest, an ambassador, who takes orders from Jesus Christ, the King over all kings.[b] It is important that you, just as all of God's children, stay closely connected to God through ongoing prayer[c] and the reading and proper application of His inspired and authoritative Word, the Bible.[d] Jesus said that His disciples would know reality and be freed from the bondage of sin if they remain in His Word following Him:[e]

---

a: (a) Luke 15:7, 10, 22-24; (b) 2 Cor 5:17-21; (c) 1 Thess 5:17; Eph 6:18; (d) 2 Tim 3:16-17; (e) John 8:31-36.

> If you remain in my word, you are truly my
> disciples, and you shall know the truth (reality),
> and the truth shall set you free.   John 8:31-32

By obediently following Jesus and reading and applying His Word, our Heavenly Father teaches Jesus' followers reality helping them break freer and freer from the diminishing sin within them. As they stay in His Word and follow His leading, He continues to bring their thinking into closer and closer alignment with His.[a]

The Father's Work & Your Development

In reality, for God's children, it is our Heavenly Father who does the final shaping and trimming,[b] and He uses the Holy Spirit to help all of Jesus' followers know His will.[c] It gives Jesus' followers great comfort to know that they are important enough to the Father that He does not give this responsibility to another. Our Heavenly Father takes primary responsibility for His obedient children's development and controls events to the point that Jesus' followers are developed properly.

As the Father makes sure that His obedient children acquire a proper understanding of the world (world-view), He develops their patience, kindness, righteousness, faithfulness, gentleness, and self control through Jesus' leadership and the indwelling of the Holy Spirit.[d] In addition to everyone being responsible to witness to those who are not following Jesus,[e] God uses Jesus' more mature followers to develop the less mature building up the entire Body of Christ.[f] We will look at Jesus' followers' development

---

a: (a) Rom 12:1-2; cf. 1 Cor 2:16; (b) John 15:1-2; (c) 1 John 2:27; Phil 2:13; (d) Gal 5:22-23; (e) John 15:1-5, 8; Matt 28:18-20; Acts 1:8; 1 Peter 2:9; (f) Eph 4:11-16; cf. 1 Cor 12:4-7.

and potential places of service within our local churches in the next chapter as we consider walking and working with God on this side of eternity until our physical death or rapture.

7

Walking with Others in the Church

Jesus said that only those who had a desire *to do the will of the Father* would come to know Him.[a] He also said that there would be some who called Him "lord" who would not be with Him in Heaven because *they had not done the Father's will.*[b] If someone wants to know God, he or she must be willing to follow His lead. God does not weigh people's good and bad activities throughout their lives to see if they have done enough good to enter Heaven. In reality, the Father only accepts people into His eternal holy family who are willing to allow Him to shape them into Jesus' moral image and obediently follow Him. *God requires commitment with corresponding action!*

Just as in Malachi's time, God wants us to trust Him enough to do our part in supporting His creative work. It is one thing to know about something, *it is something else to love God and others enough to get involved.* God asks all to listen to Him, learn to return His love, and to step out in faith and do His will.[c] *Our Creator is seeking out and working with all who love and honor Him through their actions as well as their words.*[d] Are you willing to advance by more fully doing God's will for your life? This chapter should help those who desire to know God more fully and find their personal place in His holy family experience more joy. Those who follow Jesus closely will experience more and more of His joy. It is important to remember that God only

---

a: (a) John 7:17; 8:39-47; cf. Matt 25:31-46; Rom 2:13; (b) Matt 7:21; (c) Deut 30:19-20; and others; (d) Luke 6:46; Rev 22:12.

guides those who listen to Him. If you are a follower of Jesus, God will put you to work doing your part. *Everyone is important to God and everyone who obediently listens to Him is spiritually born into His eternal holy family by Him and has a place of service.* All who listen to God come to understand that everyone is just traveling through this part of eternity (sojourning) either headed for the New Heaven and New Earth or headed for Hell.

Jesus' followers are *radically different* than the world. While His followers live out this short part of eternity, they are reminded to keep their focus on Him and His leadership versus on the many distractions of this world. They live with godly love growing in their hearts, which in turn radically alters their outlook toward others. As Jesus' followers step out in faith daily *growing in their love for God and all,*[a] they become more and more willing to suffer and sacrifice on behalf of others. In doing so, they experiencing a growing inner peace and joy.[b] *This presents a paradox to many who are not following Jesus because without a genuine love for God and others, one would normally not experience joy by helping those who normally will not pay them back for their efforts.*[c] Through Jesus' followers' individual and collective good works for all, the world has a better opportunity to understand the loving caring nature of God for all.[d]

Jesus expects His followers to help others with their needs as He leads,[e] but most importantly, He expects His followers to help others become disciples *and* grow in their relationship with God.[f] In order to do this, Jesus' followers should be intentionally seeking God's will as they help others know about God and His holy ways. *It is Jesus' followers' honor, privilege, and duty to engage people wherever they are in their spiritual journey and help them to know well the one true God.* It also important that

---

a: (a) 1 John 4:16; (b) John 15:8-11; John 17:13 & Heb 12:2; (c) John 15:12-13; 1 John 3:16-18; Col 1:24; 3:10-17; (d) Matt 5:16; Col 3:10; (e) Matt 25:34-40; (f) Matt 28:18-20; 2 Cor 5:17-21.

Jesus' followers warn people about the spiritual warfare going on around them. Everyone needs to know that Satan is still trying to deceive and hurt as many as possible.[a]

Sojourning with God

> . . . And the land shall not ever be sold because the
> land belongs to Me, (and) because you are
> temporary dwellers and sojourners with Me; . . . .
> Lev 25:23

> For ***our place of citizenship exists in (the) heavens***
> out of which we are awaiting a savior, the Lord
> Jesus Christ . . . .   Phil 3:20[b]

> Blessed is the God and Father of our lord, Jesus
> Christ, who according to His rich mercy has caused
> us ***to be born again*** into a living hope through the
> resurrection of Jesus Christ from the dead—into an
> inheritance (that is) eternal, pure, and unfading,
> which has been kept in the heavens for us, who
> through the ability of God are being guarded
> through faith for a prepared salvation that shall be
> revealed at the end of time . . . .   1 Peter 1:3-5

We are just traveling through! We are sojourning with God and one another as we join Him in rescuing as many as possible bringing them into His eternal close loving righteous family. Our interactive journey with God is fulfilling His purpose in the Creation,[c] which is to create a freewill holy family closer to

---

a: (a) 1 Peter 5:8; 2 Cor 11:13-15; (b) cf. Heb 11:8-10; (c) Eph 2:10;
2 Tim 1:8-9.

Him than His faithful angels who did not join Satan in opposing His authority.[a] When we accept God's love through Jesus Christ, we become fully reconciled children beginning our role as His priests, His representatives, His ambassadors, on earth.[b]

As God's representatives, Jesus' followers are to proclaim the reality of God's creation of an eternal intimate holy family and act as mediators between Him and the world around them. They are *not* to settle down and become satisfied using their personal talents and blessings from God solely for themselves and their families. Jesus' followers have come to recognize that their physical lives are only a small portion of their eternal lives, and that they have the honor of being co-laborers with God.[c] They have been fully reconciled to God with all the emotional and legal rights of direct descendants, and they have an eternal home with God awaiting them. They know that in a short time the good works of God, the trials, and the challenges of this age shall be over.[d] Therefore, they want to make the most of the time that God gives them on earth.

Jesus' followers have __not__ picked up passes to Heaven and are just waiting to go home, and they are __not__ presently sitting on the sidelines acting as spectators watching God at work! Jesus' followers enjoy being interactive co-laborers with the Creator.[e] *They have the privilege, honor, and duty of representing God on earth* helping fellow disciples and helping those who are living out their lives under the deceptions and leadership of Satan understand what is really happening in this world.[f] It brings Jesus' followers *great joy* to help fellow followers of Jesus and even greater joy to help rescue those who are not following Jesus from present ungodly lifestyles and future eternal shame, unrest, and suffering.[g]

---

a: (a) Rev 12:7-12; (b) Ex 19:5-6; 1 Peter 2:9-10; 2 Cor 5:17-21; (c) 1 Cor 3:9; 2 Cor 5:17-6:1; (d) Phil 3:20; Titus 2:11-14; Rev 21:1-7; (e) John 5:19; 15:5; 1 Cor 3:9; (f) 1 John 5:12, 19; 2 Cor 5:18-21; cf. John 8:34-47; (g) Rom 6:22; Rev 3:20.

Being "in Christ"

As part of the universal Church, Paul teaches that Jesus' followers are "in Christ." *Being "in Christ," means having a close obedient relationship with Jesus, God's Anointed One, the true Messiah. It is critically important to have a close relationship with Jesus in order to function well in the spiritual warfare that is constantly going on around us.* It is our obedient close association with Jesus that gives us access to the Father and enables us to overcome evil as we train some and lead others to Him.[(a)] When we faithfully follow Jesus, we come to know more fully the Father's will.[(b)]

Being "in Christ" is the only way that anyone finds true peace as they are developed more and more by the Father to have the mind of Christ.[(c)] The Holy Spirit works in all of Jesus' followers producing great love, joy, and inner peace.[(d)] Through Jesus' work through the Holy Spirit, the Father rearranges Jesus' followers' priorities, and they experience great joy being part of His great rescue operation throughout the Creation. Jesus' followers take the necessary time *to make and train* new disciples.

The Body of Christ & Godly Unity

Those who are "in Christ" are also part of the Body of Christ. Jesus is the head of the Body, the Church.[(e)] The phrase "Body of Christ" appears in the New Testament to represent Jesus' literal body or figuratively to represent His followers working together as *His bodily representatives* throughout the last part of the Creation following Jesus' resurrection.

---

a: (a) Eph 2:18; 6:10-20; (b) Phil 2:13; (c) 1 Cor 2:16; (d) Gal 5:22-24; (e) Col 1:18.

Some New Testament writers used imagery of a human body to represent the collective work of Jesus' followers as they *submit to His leadership* in order to carry out His ongoing saving work. Jesus is the head! From this metaphorical imagery, two critical attributes of Jesus' followers are highlighted:

(1) godly unity; and
(2) the synergistic ability and strength that is gained through utilization of combined individual talents being enlightened and empowered by the Father and Son through the Holy Spirit for the good of all.

In his metaphorical imagery of the Body of Christ, Paul wants all of Jesus' followers to understand the importance of each member. ***Everyone is important and has work to do under the headship of Jesus.*** When considering any physical living body, each member–whether foot, hand, ear, eye, heart, lungs, kidneys, and the list goes on–has an important contributing function to the overall ability and well being of that body.[a]

Considering how the various members of a living physical body work together for the good of the whole, Paul stressed the importance of *unity* among the various members of the Body of Christ.[b] Paul was asking the Corinthians to unite under the teaching and leadership of Jesus and follow their local teachers and leaders such as himself as individuals who were ministering directly *under* the authority of Jesus. There should be *no divisions* in any of the local churches over anything including the teachings of their distinctive local leaders such as Paul, Peter (Cephas), and Apollos. Jesus' followers were to stay *united* under *the lordship* of Jesus[c] living out holy lives.[d]

In Ephesians, Paul emphasized the importance for Gentile and Jewish Christians to treat each other as *equal family members*

---

a: (a) 1 Cor 12:12-25; (b) 1 Cor 12:26-27; cf. John 17:20-23; (c) 1 Cor 1:10-15; 3:1-8; (d) Eph 4:1-3.

disregarding the prejudices that they had learned through their various religious and cultural lives.[a] He began his teaching by using two metaphorical images to help Christians understand godly unity:

> (1) Paul used the idea that the Judean (Jewish) and Gentile Christians should be living out their lives as members of a *single* family. In this metaphorical imagery, he stated that Jesus through His death on a cross had destroyed *to mesotoichon tou phragmou*, "the dividing middle-wall," for all of His followers. This dividing middle-wall was a metaphorical image of a religious-cultural hostility that had existed for generations between Gentiles and Judeans.[b] In this metaphorical image, Paul brought to mind a common practice in the first-century Mediterranean world where some families lived in large buildings, which were subdivided into family units by "middle-walls." These "middle-walls" were solid without doors and windows providing separation for families and businesses.[59] Paul was not advocating that all of Jesus' followers live together, but he was telling Christians that they now belonged to the *same* family, the Family of God; and
> (2) Paul went on to use a second metaphorical image stating that through Jesus' redeeming work, they were all reconciled into "one body."[c]

Paul went on to explicitly state that both Judean and Gentile *Christians* were members of the same family, God's household, which made them family members and fellow citizens of His eternal kingdom.[d] He closed this important teaching on Christian unity by using one last metaphorical image. Jesus' followers could consider themselves metaphorically as individual

---

a: (a) Eph 2:11-22; (b) Eph 2:14; (c) Eph 2:16; (d) Eph 2:19.

parts of the great House of God, which is continually under construction until the last person is added.[a] Through Jesus, the holy family of God can now experience peace within itself despite their various backgrounds.[b]

The Church

The Greek word *ekklēsia*, which was understood in the first century as "assembly," is now normally being translated by many as "church." First century "assemblies" normally referred to called meetings whether religious, political, or general. Paul taught the various assemblies that met in homes, synagogues, and other structures,[c] *that the risen Lord Jesus was still the active lord of the world-wide Church.*[d] He told Jesus' followers at Corinth, "You are the Body of Christ, indeed *a member of a part of the whole* [1 Cor 12:27]." The followers at Corinth were a part of their local assemblies, which resided in their region, which was a part of the entire world-wide Body, the universal Church.[e]

After Jesus died on the Cross for all humanity and ascended into Heaven to rule at His Father's right hand,[f] we see a major shift from the national Israel's religious leaders to God's people, the new Israel, consisting of all who became faithful followers of the one true Messiah, Jesus.[g] Within the first twenty years after Jesus' ascension, many Gentiles had begun following Israel's long awaited prophesied Messiah (Christ).[h] Within thirty years, Paul said that the Gospel had been made known to all nations,[i] which shows that many Gentiles of various nations had already heard the Good News about what God had done through His Son, Jesus. Just as Jesus had prophesied to Israel's religious leaders of His day, the Father had removed their authority and given it to another group of

---

a: (a) Eph 2:20-22; (b) Eph 2:14; (c) Heb 10:23-25; (d) Col 1:18; (e) 1 Cor 12:28; (f) Eph 1:18-23; (g) Gal 6:16; Phil 3:3; cf. Matt 21:33-45; (h) Acts 15:3; (i) Rom 16:26.

leaders and people, who now consisted of Jews (Judeans) and Gentiles[a] who actively followed Jesus. As part of God's plan, He allowed Israel's Temple to be destroyed by the Romans in A.D. 70. This removed the nation of Israel's central place of leadership and worship, which fulfilled Jesus' declaration that God was now seeking His obedient children to worship Him in spirit and truth.[b]

With Jesus' ascension to sit at the right hand of the Father, He became known as the King of Peace and Eternal High Priest.[c] When the Creation is finished, everyone–saved and unsaved–will submit to the lordship of Christ, who after judging, will in turn hand everything over to the Father in order that everyone will recognize the Father as the overall leader of everything.[d]

During Jesus' present reign over the Heavens and Earth, the Church, His Body, represents Him on Earth. The Church is no longer obligated to keep the nation Israel's ordinances that regulated Israel's cultural norms[e] nor the sacrificial laws, which were fulfilled through Christ's atoning death.[f] This allows the Church to follow the eternal moral lifestyle of God within all cultures as long as those cultural practices do not violate God's moral standards.[g] Wherever God's people live, they are expected to live according to His moral standards caring for all.[h]

Denominational, racial, generational, socio-economical, and political walls have all been constructed through Satan's prompting as humanity with its abundant free will has struggled against God, His authority, and His good plans for everyone. Jesus' followers should be dismantling these walls within their local churches and their cultures as they live out their lives. It is important that we, Jesus' followers, learn to take pleasure in allowing our Heavenly Father to teach our hearts to love as He

---

a: (a) Matt 21:43; (b) John 4:21-24; (c) Heb 7:1-8:6; (d) 1 Cor 11:3; 15:28; cf. John 14:28; (e) Acts 15:4-21; Eph 2:13-16; Col 2:9-23; (f) Heb 7:26-27; 8:13; 10:4, 10-14; (g) Rom 2:11-16; 3:31; 6:1-2; 7:12; (h) Eph 4:1-6; 1 Peter 1:17-19.

loves as we learn to live together as members of the same eternal holy family. The universal Church is the part of God's eternal holy family that is presently living on Earth. It needs to act accordingly.

Walking with Others in Our Local Churches

The Church first and foremost is the holy Family of God! All true followers of Jesus Christ are part of the same Kingdom and have the same Sustainer living in them.[a] Jesus' followers worldwide and locally must allow Jesus to teach them more fully about God's holy family and its final state with perfect godly unity, "oneness," which became reality through His death as the world's sacrificial lamb.[b] All of Jesus' followers should be presently striving for a high level of godly unity.

Members of local churches everywhere in the world should be so caring for one another that they are able to share important thoughts with one another without worrying about sensitive information being used against them at later times to cause harm. Due to unbelief and immaturity, many within local churches still hurt each other on a regular basis. But, for those who are mature followers of Jesus, the door is open for a rich relationship with other true followers of Jesus. Wouldn't it be great if Jesus' followers could learn to care enough about one another to live in transparency and not hurt each other bringing additional joy and inner peace to their lives?

Within each local church, Jesus should be producing inner peace and joy in the hearts of its members. If there is little peace and joy, you and your fellow members need to fast and pray seeking God's help in removing sin and walking more closely with Him until He gives you a breakthrough. Members of congregations who are walking closely with God *will* experience great love, joy, inner peace, and excitement as people continually come to God

---

a: (a) Eph 4:1-6; (b) John 1:29; 4:42; 17:20-23.

through their ministry and grow in their relationship with God and one another.

Being Social

As godly social beings, we should be volunteering in order *to do our part* within the holy Family of God. When members of the family are all doing their part, things go more smoothly and everyone experiences more godly unity and joy. Consider living at home for a moment. Think of the importance of parents teaching their children to do their part. If children do not learn to help with the basic work around the house and yard, they hinder their families and grow up with a personal handicap in managing and taking care of their own future families. It is important within families for each capable member to do his or her part. If some are not socially responsible in helping, others have to do more than they should. This takes away from other areas of the lives of the overworked causing them and the entire family to suffer. This is contrary to God's desire for our personal families, His local church families, and even His world-wide Holy Family, the universal Church. If we are not experiencing some level of godly unity within our local churches, we should seek our Heavenly Father's help in learning the importance of following Jesus' leadership. *It is only through our obedience to Jesus' leadership that we will learn to work together in a godly fashion.* If Jesus does not hold first place within our own hearts and the hearts of our local church leaders, it does not take long for our churches to become self-seeking and ineffective individually and collectively.

Knowing and Employing My Talents

It is God who is working in you (pl.) to desire and
to work according to His good purpose.   Phil 2:13

We are His doing, having been created in Christ
Jesus for good works, which God has prepared
ahead of time in order that we may live out our lives
accordingly.   Eph 2:10[a]

*If a person willingly follows Jesus, our heavenly Father
will give that individual a desire and the ability to do His
predetermined assignments.* Each person in God's holy family has
assignments to help our local church families and our universal
Church family function more smoothly. God has gifted each person
with special skills so that when Jesus' followers utilize their
diversity properly, the Family of God operates in a productive
manner through the empowerment of the Holy Spirit.[b] The
combined output of everyone working under the lordship of Jesus
is much greater than the sum of all individual work (synergism).
This is true on local church levels and on our combined
international level through the universal Church.

Every position within God's holy family is important. God
has no favorites and all of His children are loved just as He loves
Jesus.[c] Therefore, enjoy whatever God has appointed you to do.
Remember, it is God who has created you with unique talents, and
if you are willing to follow Jesus, it is the Father who gives you the
ability through the Holy Spirit to fulfill your part of the Creation.[d]

Each of Christ's disciples should be *seeking God's perfect
will* for their lives so that they may grow into effective, loving co-
members of their respective local churches. Each should seek
God's will to find his or her place within their local assemblies so
that their local churches may be working at peak performance in
their local, regional, national, and world-wide ministries. As each
of Jesus' followers pick up their individual crosses following His

a: (a) cf. James 2:14-26; (b) 1 Cor 12:12-27; cf. Acts 1:7-8; (c) John
17:23; (d) Phil 2:13.

lead, they will learn how to utilize best their individual talents helping one another and witnessing with godly effective power to the world. Each true follower of Jesus is a new creation[a] undergoing constant training in righteousness by our Heavenly Father through the Holy Spirit and other members of his or her local church and/or universal Church (sanctification).[b]

My Gifts/Talents

So what about your gifts/talents from God. Many of you have already figured out what you are good at and what you are not. Nevertheless, if you are still struggling with understanding your God-given talents, there are many fairly straight forward spiritual tests available that show individuals their overall strengths and weaknesses. But, keep in mind that you should not let any test result become your automatic guide to service within your local church and beyond. ***Pray and ask God to reveal His desire for your work, and He will initiate a desire in your heart*** to do what He has assigned you to accomplish. It may not match your greatest apparent skills. In reality, skills are important, but without Jesus no one can do any spiritual work effectively. The spiritual battles around us are too great for humanity without God's leading and empowerment.

Paul taught the Corinthians, that although everyone was not a great evangelist, preacher, or teacher, all had an important part in Christ's Body.[c] Some are carpenters, others cooks, others accountants, and the list goes on. But the one task that all of Jesus' followers have is the privilege, honor, and duty of sharing the Good News about God and His ongoing creation of a close-knit holy family. All of His family living on earth has the joy, honor,

---

a: (a) 2 Cor 5:17; (b) John 15:1-2; Rom 6:22; Gal 5:22-23; (c) 1 Cor 12:11-31.

and responsibility of helping others know God and His Creation (witnessing).

Your journey with God starts with submission to Jesus and continues when you step out in faith and find your place of service within the Body. After submitting to Jesus' leadership and committing to live according to God's Word, *the last major part in your beginning walk with God is for you to step out in faith (trust) and participate within the Church helping to grow His eternal close-knit holy family.* As you seek God's will in prayer, reading of His word, and talking to others, consider how you might bless your local church and others through God's calling on your life. Do not be afraid of starting on a wrong path, because if you somehow misunderstand God's calling and start helping in an area that was not meant for you, God will help you move to a more appropriate place of service. It is a lot easier for God to help you find a closer match to His plan for your life if you are serving in some capacity rather than if you are doing nothing.

Empowerment as Needed

In his book, *The Journey*, Billy Graham reminds everyone that when one submits to God's lordship they are not alone. *When someone submits to Jesus Christ as lord and savior, God gives them a whole new destiny with a new purpose and power.* Jesus' followers are given a *new life*. This new life includes a *new relationship* with Him and others as a member of His eternal holy family and citizenship in the Kingdom of Heaven.[60]

If we are following Jesus, God will empower us to carry out our assigned ministries. In reality, spiritual battles are beyond our capability without Jesus leading the way and empowering us. Through Jesus Christ and the indwelling of the Holy Spirit, the Father supplies the appropriate authority, power, resources, talent, and frame of mind to each and every one of Jesus' followers. *It is the Father and Son's empowerment working through the Holy Spirit that enables Jesus' disciples to work together effectively and joyfully.*[a] It is the Holy Spirit, who enlightens and works in each of Jesus' disciples as they bring a lost world to God through their actions and words.[b]

Stepping Out in Faith

God asks each of Jesus' followers to help others on an individual, family, local-church, and community-wide level as part of their *daily* lives. Although our Heavenly Father is not asking all of Jesus' followers to go into full-time ministry, He is asking *all* to step out in faith and become involved. As followers of Jesus listen to Him, they do their assigned parts helping their local church families proclaim the Gospel. Through prayer, seeking utilization of godly talent, and ministering under Jesus and His appointed local overseers, our Heavenly Father helps Jesus' followers serve others individually and collectively.

Once an individual has made a genuine commitment to follow Jesus Christ, there is only one thing left to do: *do it!* We are justified and empowered only when we *trust and obey* the Sent Son. Therefore, let us *joyfully do* our assigned works, not out of resentment nor fear but out of a growing love for God and others. It is critical for Jesus' followers *to step out in faith and actually follow Him. Implementation matters!*

---

a: (a) Acts 1:8; Eph 3:16, 20; Phil 4:13; 2 Tim 1:7; cf. Eph 6:10-18;
(b) Rom 8:14; 1 Cor 2:13; Eph 1:13; 2 Tim 1:14.

Consider this potential personal scenario:

> (1) you see a vegetable stand on the side of the road selling incredibly good fresh local grown vegetables at 80% off local market pricing;
> (2) you seize the opportunity and purchase some fresh vegetables for the rest of the week thinking about how good fresh salads and steamed vegetables will be for your health;
> (3) you take your fresh vegetables home and put them away planning on using them starting the very next day; and
> (4) you never take the time to make the first salad nor steam the first pan of vegetables, and they all spoil.

What type of benefit did you get from buying those fresh vegetables and planning for good? Do you see the problem? Desiring something and even investing in something does not mean that you will benefit from your planning and investing. There are many people who have all sorts of good plans and investments such as exercise machines and self help books just collecting dust. *If you do not follow through and implement your plans and investments, they will never do you any good!*

This is the same phenomena that is continually occurring in our contemporary local churches. Many are meeting on a regular basis with others and making plans to get serious about their walk with Jesus. But, through Satan's deceptions, personal desires, and many forms of busyness most do not implement their commitment by stepping out in faith and truly following Jesus. In their book, *Beyond Belief to Convictions*, Josh McDowell and Bob Hostetler state that if individuals do not follow through on something that inspires them within hours after inspiration, many forget and move on as if nothing had occurred.[61] When you are inspired by God and realize that you should make a change in your life, make a commitment to follow God's lead and quickly step out in faith to live accordingly.

Jesus' Followers Are on Mission

Through Jesus Christ, God has fulfilled His promise to all by making it possible for everyone to be blessed through Abraham, who walked in faithful obedience with Him.[a] When Jesus carried out His mission by coming to us on our human level and proclaiming God's great love and righteousness through His actions and words, He fulfilled our shortcomings by living perfectly according to the Father's instructions for godly living (the Law) and dying an atoning death on the Cross for all.[b] He made God's perfect unity possible for all who receive Him,[c] and since His resurrection, He has been guiding the Church to reveal His Father's creative plan more fully than ever before to those on Earth and in Heaven.[d]

God's plan of rescuing all people from the corruption of sin had been hidden from everyone including Satan and his evil coworkers from the beginning of the Creation.[e] *The overall Gospel Message clearly proclaims that all who freely receive the Father's Sent Son, Jesus, and submit to His leadership are fully reconciled to Him for eternity.* They are born spiritually into His eternal close-knit holy family and join God as He carries out His great rescue mission.[f]

Being Light

Jesus' mission is also His followers' mission. Jesus is the Light of the World: He exposes reality.[g] After Jesus' ascension, His disciples, *the Church, became the light of the world.*[h] They

---

a: (a) Gen 12:1-4; 15:6; cf. Heb 11:8-12; (b) John 3:14-17; 13:1; Gal 3:13-14; (c) John 1:11-13; 17:20-23; cf. Rev 3:20; (d) Eph 3:9-11; (e) Col 1:26-28; (f) 1 Peter 5:8-9; 2 Cor 11:13-15; (g) John 8:12; 8:31b-32; 18:37; (h) Matt 5:14.

do not minister alone. Jesus and the Father dwell in them through the Holy Spirit providing guidance and empowerment as needed.[a] If individuals reject Jesus' followers, they are in reality rejecting the Father and Son.[b] Jesus promised not to leave His followers alone, and therefore, sent the Holy Spirit, the Helper, to guide them in all truth speaking to them the words of the Father.[c]

Jesus' earthly life gives everyone a perfect presentation of His Heavenly Father's nature.[d] Jesus' earthly life presented a visible *image* (nature) of the invisible Father.[e] If you knew Jesus during His earthly life, you had seen the very nature of His Heavenly Father at work.[f] Prior to disobeying God and being corrupted by sin, Adam and Eve were created in the image of the Father and Son.[g] Jesus' followers, the Church, are being renewed into the *image* of Jesus and the Father.[h] When Jesus' followers act like Jesus, the World sees the nature of God through them. The Church led by Jesus through the Holy Spirit is the Father's only physical representation on earth.[i] Jesus' followers should represent God well *being bright godly light*. Bright light reveals reality; dim light allows much to be hidden.

I heard a story one time about a blind lady who worked at an airport making a living selling merchandise. One day being in a great hurry, a traveler knocked over her stand with all its merchandise. He was in such a hurry that he did not even stop to help her put her stand up nor make any effort to help her recover her merchandise, which had been scattered everywhere. Everyone else seemed equally in a rush and the blind lady managed by herself to straighten her stand and then started crawling about on the floor feeling for her merchandise. She was emotionally distraught as she tried to recover her merchandise in the midst of such a hectic crowd. Finally, a traveler seeing her plight stopped

---

a: (a) John 14:23; Acts 1:8; 1 John 3:9; (b) Luke 10:16; (c) John 16:7, 13; (d) Heb 1:3; Col 2:9; (e) Col 1:15; (f) John 14:9; (g) Gen 1:26; (h) Col 3:10; (i) Col 2:10; 2 Cor 5:17-21.

and took the time to help her gather all of her merchandise and helped her place it in the stand. She thanked him for helping and asked him a simple question prior to his departure, "are you Jesus?" How many opportunities do we miss on a regular basis because we are so self absorbed or just too busy to take the time to show others Jesus through our actions and words?

Initially, Jesus' followers waited together for empowerment from God, which occurred on Pentecost, the Feast of First-Fruits.[a] *After being empowered*, they ministered together with one heart and mind providing a great witness,

> All those who were trusting (God) were together
> and had all things common, and were selling and
> dividing their possessions and property (giving) to
> each one according to whatever he or she had need;
> and throughout each day they were together of one
> mind in the Temple, and breaking bread from house
> to house, receiving (eating) food *with great joy* and
> humility of heart praising God and having grace
> toward all people. And the Lord was placing those
> who were being saved throughout each day together.
>
> Acts 2:44-47

They did not sell *all* their possessions, *nor* was it mandatory to sell any of their possessions to be part of the Church.[b] In reality, Jesus' first-century followers still had personal property including homes, yet they had relinquished their personal ownership of all over to God.[c] They were striving to be good stewards of everything under their personal authority.

We observe that as Jesus' followers were filled with the Holy Spirit (born from above, born of the Spirit), they were willing

---

a: (a) Acts 1:8, 14; 2:1-47; (b) Example: Acts 5:4; (c) cf. Luke 14:33.

to share more with others. A proper relationship with God, which is built on love, taught them to be genuinely concerned for people who were not part of their immediate biological families. Jesus gave everything including His life to help *everyone*. Jesus is still giving of Himself to lead the Church. Out of a growing love for God and others, Jesus' followers are learning to give as the Father and Son give. Many of Jesus' early followers lived out a close-knit unity with one heart and mind.[a] As they learned to love more and more as God loves, they naturally followed Jesus' lead working as "one" in godly unity within His holy family.[b]

As Jesus' followers proclaimed God's love, they were in reality proclaiming His holiness, which is His loving righteous way of life. Love and righteousness go hand-in-hand.[c] God's love for all establishes His standards of righteousness. God's righteous standards also bring about wrath (judgment) concluding in death (eternal separation from God) for all who reject Him and His loving holy way of life.[d]

Therefore, in order to proclaim the Gospel–like Jesus' closest first-century disciples–*Jesus' present day followers must declare God's holiness as part of the Gospel Message.* The Gospel declares God's love and righteous work on everyone's behalf along with His desire for everyone to turn to Him in order to be saved from the consequences of sin, which brings corruption and eternal judgment.[e] Sin must be forsaken and eventually eradicated. The whole purpose of Jesus' atoning death is to provide purification (justification) for those learning to return God love so that they are able to live with Him within His eternal holy family.[f] Living in loving righteousness (holiness) without sin is what makes eternal peace possible in the New Heaven. God's children will be morally perfected to match God's moral perfection.[g]

---

a: (a) Acts 2:42f; 4:32f; (b) John 17:11, 20-23; (c) Matt 22:37-40; Gal 5:14; (d) Rom 6:23; (e) Rom 1:16-17; 6:1-7; 8:21; (f) 2 Cor 5:17-21; Col 2:13-14; (g) Lev 19:2; Rev 22:14-15.

Jesus' followers should be engaging their cultures in order to introduce God and His phenomenal plan for the Creation to all who will listen. The New Testament is full of historical occurrences where Jesus' followers helped many realize that their lives were not being lived out optimally unless they were listening to God. They helped them know God, His holy ways, and His plan for an eternal perfected loving family. Over the centuries, many others have followed Jesus and have also proclaimed the Father's righteousness and good plans for all who would listen. *Just as the generations before us, our generation must do the same!*

It is never easy to take a firm stand where you live or travel and proclaim God's loving-kind righteousness to people who are enjoying sin, which only lasts for a season. Sin produces corruption and eventual death, if one does not eventually turn to God. Not only will Jesus' true followers be unpopular much of the time, there will be times when Satan will encourage those not following God to persecute those who are. But, as Paul taught, if Jesus' followers do not proclaim the Good News about God and His desired outcome for the Creation (Gospel Message), how will those traveling on the Wide-Road that leads to eternal separation from God understand what is really going on?[a]

Developing & Multiplying Disciples

> And Christ gave on the one hand apostles, but on the other prophets, evangelists, pastors, and teachers for the establishing of His Holy Ones (Saints) for the work of the Ministry for the building up of the Body of Christ, until we all come, to the unity of faith and knowledge of the Son of God, to a perfect (complete) man, to a measure of the maturity of the fulness of Christ.　　　　　Eph 4:11-13

a: (a) Rom 10:14.

As we come to the place of wanting Jesus to lead us, He helps us know and do the good works that our Heavenly Father set for each of us during the planning stages of the Creation. A great part of that work is developing God's holy family so that Jesus' followers can collectively take care of one another and become productive helpful witnesses. God wants those who are more mature in His family to help train those who are less mature. After leading people to Jesus, it is very important that the more mature teach the less mature how to live out *all* that Jesus commanded.

In his book, *The Journey*, Billy Graham reminds us that people who have recently turned to follow Christ are in reality like newborn children regarding their understanding of spiritual things.[62] There may be barriers to spiritual growth such as continuing sin, ungodly pressure from family members, friends, or associates, or uncertainty in what is expected.[63] Jesus' more mature followers should be teaching and guiding those who are less mature (mentorship). It is a privilege for the more mature to help the less mature grow more and more into the likeness of Christ.

It is Jesus' more mature followers' *duty, honor, and privilege* to help those who are less mature grow in their understanding and walk with Him and others.[a] Jesus' more mature followers should provide regular times of collective worship, small group meetings, Bible studies, specialized discipleship classes, and times of active ministry to help the entire Body grow. If the mature members of our local churches do not help make and develop new disciples *including their own children*, how will future generations know God and His way of life?

---

a: (a) Matt 28:20; Acts 2:42.

Being Committed

It takes courage and commitment to step out in faith and teach God's Word when it is unpopular, but under God's leadership and empowerment, some will listen and be saved. A German, Dietrich Bonhoeffer, was a faithful follower of Jesus during the years leading up to and during WWII and was martyred in a concentration camp located at Flossenburg on April 9, 1945 just before the end of the war in Europe.[64] Bonhoeffer's life was one of engaging his culture and speaking out against the terrible things that Hitler and many of the German leaders were doing. Many of his own countrymen would not speak out against Hitler either because of fear of loss including their lives or possible loss of personal gain that might be obtained by following him.

Bonhoeffer called many of His countryman to task for not following Christ's teachings and wrote a book titled *The Cost of Discipleship* reminding people that following Jesus required commitment and action.[65] As life became more difficult for him in prison, Bonhoeffer came to realize that following Jesus depended wholeheartedly on turning one's life over to God. He came to realize that repentance was a true turning to God and that Jesus' followers need to live life out trusting God *unreservedly* in all circumstances. *By turning to God and depending on Him fully, one became a true follower of Jesus, a renewed man of God.* He came to realize that God—no matter what the circumstances—would lead him and all of Jesus' followers home to Himself.[66]

8

—

Helping Others Know God

Jesus, "In this way my Father is glorified: that you
bear much fruit indeed being my disciples."

John 15:8

In reality, as Jesus' followers live out their lives being led
by Jesus through the Holy Spirit,[a] they reveal their Heavenly
Father's glory that is full of grace and truth through their actions as
well as their words. As Jesus' followers help others to know God,
some who have not yet come to know Him come to realize that the
Father, Son, and Holy Spirit are caring, righteous, and full of grace
and truth with abundant loving-kindness toward all. *They are truly
glorious!*

As Jesus' followers proclaim God's loving nature to a
world that is engulfed in many deceptions and corrupted by sin,
some come to realize that God is worthy to follow, and they turn
from Satan and his deceptions to God for a much better life now
and forever. It is critical for those following Jesus to remember that
spiritual warfare is ongoing with the devil (Satan),[b] who wants to
separate as many as possible from God.[c] The Son of God
constantly opposes Satan and leads all who will listen against him.
It is through His atoning death on everyone's behalf that Jesus has
made it possible for God's obedient children of all ages to have a
future eternal sinless life.[d] Knowing how good God is makes it a

---

a: (a) Rom 8:14; (b) Eph 6:10-12; (c) John 8:44; (d) John 10:9-11; cf.
Rom 6:22-23.

joy and an honor for me to help people know the Father and Son more fully knowing that when someone listens to God on any real level, their life will improve now and forever.

As Jesus' followers work together, we should be confident in God's ability, and we should celebrate the fact that we are able to do the greatest works of the Creation because of Jesus' ongoing leadership and His finished atoning work.[a] Just as Jesus called many from the first century into obedient discipleship, He continues to call obedient disciples from every successive generation to proclaim the good news of His growing eternal holy family and kingdom. Jesus' followers know that the Gospel message is empowered by God through the Holy Spirit and is working in everyone's life including their own.[b] They know that God's way of life is the only way whereby people can find inner peace and godly joy now and forever.[c]

The Church's Main Mission

The Father's main mission is also His family's main mission. The Father's main mission for His Creation is to bring as many as will obediently listen to Him into His eternal close-knit loving righteous (holy) family.[d] With the great level of freedom that the Father has given everyone, He desires that all come to a place of turning from their individual desires and aspirations to Him and His way of life.[e] Those who listen and learn to return His love become part of His eternal holy family.[f] Jesus' followers do their part in helping those who are not listening to God start listening by openly displaying God's goodness through their actions as well as their words. If those who normally are not listening start to realize how good God is, they have a better chance

---

a: (a) John 14:12; cf. John 7:37-39; (b) Rom 1:16; Col 1:3-6; (c) Rom 6:22-23; 7:4; 8:23; (d) John 3:16-17; 2 Peter 3:9; (e) Matt 11:28-30; Luke 9:23; 2 Peter 3:9; (f) 1 John 4:10-19.

of paying attention to the teaching and leading of Jesus through the Holy Spirit as well as listening to Jesus' followers.

Keep in mind that God has not made any mistakes by giving an enormous amount of freedom to His children, which resulted in great sin and corruption. The Crown Jewel of His Creation is His finalized eternal loving close righteous ***mutually-interactive*** family. Prior to the Creation being implemented physically, He had correspondingly put in place a plan to remove all sin from those who listened to Him. Within this plan, His Son, Jesus, understood His part to become incarnate and journey with man for a little while teaching truth (reality) and eventually dying on a cross in order to provide sin removal for all who would learn to obediently listen to the Father throughout the entire Creation.[a] This is the same Jesus who spoke the universe into existence under the Father's guidance.[b]

When Nicodemus, a religious leader, came to Jesus to understand His messianic saving work, Jesus told him that ***it was necessary for one to be born a second time through the Holy Spirit in order to see and enter the Kingdom of God.***[c] He went on to tell Nicodemus that ***it was necessary that He, the Son of God, die in order that those who were trusting God could be born a second time providing salvation.***[d] This would be their spiritual birth into God's holy family. He went on say that His Heavenly Father loves everyone so much that He had sent His Son, Jesus, into the world at just the right time to do just that.[e] As Jesus came to the point of completing the main part of His mission and dying for all,[f] He prayed that His followers would experience the fulness of joy that He was experiencing ***as He looked beyond*** the pain and humiliation of dying on a cross to the salvation that He was making available for everyone who learned to trust God.[g]

---

a: (a) 1 John 4:10-19; (b) Heb 1:2; cf. John 1:1-3; (c) John 3:3, 5; (d) John 3:14-15; (e) John 3:16-17; Gal 4:4-5; (f) John 13:1, 3; (g) John 15:5, 11;17:13; Heb 12:2; cf. Heb 10:4-14.

Knowing God's love for all and His desired outcome of this Creation helps Jesus' followers willing lay aside some of their personal goals and become faithful witnesses as they join God in His creative work. As Jesus' followers (disciples) learn to hear and obey His voice more fully, they have a closer and closer relationship with the Father, Jesus, the Holy Spirit, and one another, and they become much more effective in witnessing. As they step out in faith and follow Jesus, they realize that there are many within their own families, local churches, and local communities who also need to start following Jesus. These people become their *daily* mission fields. Everyone needs to know that God is real and loves them more than they love themselves, but He also has a loving righteous way of life that must be followed. It is a privilege and honor for Jesus' followers to represent God showing through their actions and words His very nature.[a] One of Max Lucado's books, *Out Live Your Life: You Were Made To Make a Difference*, offers some sound reflection with practical examples on how Jesus' followers are able to help others know God better.[67]

There is no greater joy than helping save those whom you are learning to love dearly from a present life of continual ongoing sin with its consequences and an eternal life of shame, unrest, and suffering. If you are following Jesus, you will experience joy with God as you lead others to Him. There is rejoicing in Heaven over every person who decides to receive God into their lives.[b]

If you desire to experience more love, joy, and inner peace, *let God show you the spiritual importance of your participation in helping to build His eternal caring family and kingdom.* God shows all who listen the importance of submitting to His will, putting aside personal ambitions (dying to self), and receiving the mind of Christ, which allows one to experience Jesus' joy as they help others turn to God.[c] Paul uses the idea of "having been

---

a: (a) Matt 25:34-40; 28:18-20; (b) Luke 15:7, 10, 31-32; (c) 1 Cor 2:7, 12, 16.

crucified with Christ" to help express the idea of giving up one's personal ambitions and desires in order to help the world know Him.[a] Paul's dying to self and suffering on behalf of those who would listen to God brought him great joy.[b] This is the same for all who follow Jesus.

Jesus' life was fulfilled by pleasing His Heavenly Father.[c] He experienced great levels of inner peace and joy through consistently and obediently remaining in His Father's love. Jesus' followers may also experience this great inner peace and joy by obediently remaining in Jesus' love.[d] As we each consider how God might use us to impact others for Him, it is good to keep in mind that each one of us has a limited amount of time during our physical life in order to help others know God. So, it is good to seek God's help to know what our preassigned good works are.[e] Let's please God by giving back to Him for some of the good that He constantly does for us. Let's help others know how good God is including His great love and patience for all as we all work together to bring as many as possible into His and our eternal loving righteous family.

The Great Commission Is a Work of Love

Prior to His ascension to rule Heaven and Earth under the direction of His Father, Jesus gave His immediate and all future disciples a charge, a commission:

All authority in Heaven and on Earth has been given to me. Therefore, while living out your lives, *make disciples* of all nations, baptizing them in the name of the Father, the Son, and the Holy Spirit, teaching

---

a: (a) Gal 2:19-20; (b) Col 1:24; (c) John 4:34; (d) John 15:10; (e) Eph 2:10.

them to keep all that I commanded you.
And behold! I am with you all every day until the
total completion of the Age.   Matt 28:18-20

During this Age of Grace, the Messianic Age, Jesus commands all of His followers to make disciples from *all* people groups of the world. *Originating out of God's love for all, this is the one overarching command given to all of Jesus' followers.*

As Jesus' followers live out their lives daily learning to love God and their fellow man more fully, they proclaim the Gospel Message, the Good News, through their *actions as well as their words* and help develop disciples from all who receive Jesus as lord and savior. *Each of Jesus' followers have the honor and privilege of participating with God in His ongoing Creation* inviting all to receive Him and join His eternal close-knit holy family. Through Jesus Christ's ongoing leadership among His followers and the convicting work of the Holy Spirit,[a] new followers are continually added to God's eternal holy family as they start listening and learning to love, trust, and obey God due to His unbiased great love for all and His ability to carry out His promises.

God encourages all of us through Paul's writings to remember that Jesus' followers are also His ambassadors (representatives)[b] taking the Good News of God's creation of an eternal sinless family to all who will listen and receive Him into their personal lives. When we are telling others the Good News of God's Creation, it is important to keep in mind that God gives everyone a great amount of freedom requesting that each consider what He is requesting and then make a decision either to receive or reject Him and His way of life. Although Adam and Eve disobeyed God fairly early on within the Creation resulting in sin, corruption,

---

a: (a) John 16:7-11; cf. Rom 2:11-16; (b) 2 Cor 5:20.

and chaos for all,[a] God wants everyone to make their own choices having experienced both good and bad. The Good News includes the idea that the abundant freedom that God gave His created children, which initially resulted in great sin, made it possible for a voluntary eternal mutually-interactive sinless family.

Within God's eternal close-knit equalitarian family, there are no longer any ethnic nor social distinctions.[b] In Ephesians 2:11-22, we see that Jesus' death on a cross tore down the ethnic and cultural wall of hostility between the Jews (Israel) and the rest of the world for all who become part of God's eternal holy family.[68] There have been people throughout the Creation, who have allowed Satan to deceive them into thinking that the God whom Israel followed and proclaimed to the world was a God who heavily favored Israel over the rest of the world. This is incorrect, which can be shown to be false by considering some of the key interactions of God with man including the overall Good News proclamation starting with God's promise to Abraham that *all of the world* would be blessed through him.[c] Later, after freeing Israel from slavery in Egypt, Yahweh, the Creator, told Israel that if they wanted Him to be their god (sustainer), they would become His priests (representatives) to the world.[d]

Therefore, as we help people know God better, keep in mind that the people whom you talk to about God may come from an assortment of religious, cultural, and/or socio-economical backgrounds. Satan is behind all teachings that produce other gods and philosophies, and he does this in order to lead people away from the one true Creator God. All of Satan's alternatives encourage people to ignore the Creator, the One True God, and help them justify self-centeredness, which helps enslave people to him and their sin through their unholy actions (sin).

---

a: (a) Rom 8:18-23; (b) Gal 3:28; (c) Gen 12:3c; 18:17-19; (d) Exod 19:4-9.

A good example of satanic deception can be found in the writings of a fourth century Roman emperor, Julian (Flavius Claudius Iulianus), who like many over the ages bought into a lie stating that the God of Israel was not the God of all people. Because of Satan's deceptions, he wrote against Jesus Christ and the Church through his written work, *Against the Galileans.*[69] Yahweh, the God of Israel, created all people, loves all people, and makes available to all the possibility of living a sinless eternal life with Him. As we talk to people about God, it is important to remember that God loves all people and wants everyone to receive Him into their lives.[a] When witnessing, we should ask the Holy Spirit to help us know the best way to help each individual see the reality of past satanic deceptions and understand more fully how much God loves them personally.

Witnessing for Jesus

Through Jesus' leading of the Church through the Holy Spirit,[b] God continually works in His Creation teaching the truth of His great love for all and the importance of following His holy way of life. As we discussed earlier, God has a spiritual connection with all people starting at conception and helps them to know reality but still allows the great deceiver to tempt everyone to live life the way that they want and ignore their Creator. Many people are satisfied with a life where God is not their lord failing to realize that along with God's lordship comes a better life that is filled with a growing love, joy, and inner peace. They fail to realize that what God wants for each is based on what is best for each instead of Satan and his deceptions, which leads to a lesser quality life ending with eternal separation from God and His holy family.

a: (a) 2 Peter 3:9; cf. John 3:16; (b) Rom 2:11-16; cf. John 16:7-11; Acts 1:6-8.

Even while under great duress and persecution at times, Jesus' first-century followers helped as many as would listen see past Satan's deceptions in order that they might see and acknowledge the realty of our loving Creator.[a] ***Every generation including our own must do the same even at a high cost!*** We must come to understand within our hearts as well as our minds that ***eternal separation from God is the worst thing that can happen to anyone***. As we come to understand the importance of Jesus' command ***to make disciples***, it becomes apparent that we should understand some of the basics of sharing the truth of God's Creation with others.

Effective witnessing starts with a genuine concern about others and then a willingness ***to share Life*** with anyone God puts before us as we go about our everyday lives.[b] Jesus teaches us that as we learn to trust and obey Him out of love (not fear), we will do even greater works than He did while ministering on earth because He is now with the Father leading us.[c] It is our privilege and honor to introduce God to others praying that they will see His goodness and receive Him into their lives.

Sometimes in our busy world, we forget that the most important work that we can do is to help others know God. So let's continue on today in the footsteps of Jesus' first-century followers continuing to work hard to make God known and rejoicing with God as some of the lost start following Jesus.

Intentional Witnessing

The Father works with His Son, the Holy Spirit, and His Son's followers of every generation to help everyone know the

---

a: (a) Examples: Col 1:24; cf. 2 Cor 4:7-11; 16-18; 1 Peter 1:6-9; Heb 10:32-39; and others; (b) John 14:6; (c) John 14:12.

reality of His Creation including His redeeming work available to all:

(1) through *the Holy Spirit's personal teaching* about life and the Creation;[a]
(2) through *the Holy Spirit's convicting teaching* regarding sin, righteousness, and the judgment to come;[b] and
3) through *Jesus and His followers' teaching* about God, His loving righteous way of life, and His helpful Word, which provides opportunities for everyone to know God better; Jesus' followers teach through their actions as well as their words.[c]

As Christ's followers share the Gospel (the Good News) with those not following Jesus and teach about: (1) God's love, (2) free will, (3) personal sin, (4) God's redeeming work, and (5) personal repentance, each one hearing the Gospel is personally responsible for their response. As Jesus' followers share the Good News about what God is doing through His Creation, some will experience moments of spiritual awakening. During these moments, individuals have an opportunity to realize the damaging effect of personal sin and make a conscious decision to turn from their self-centered and selfish ways to God and His loving righteous ways (repentance). Even if some do not want to listen to the Father during their spiritual awakening moments, they are required to consider Him and His way of life including the cost of submitting to Him and following Jesus. Eventually, everyone must personally decide to either receive or reject Him; making no decision to follow Jesus is the same as rejecting the Father.[d]

---

a: (a) Rom 1:18-32; 2:11-16; cf. 1 John 2:27; (b) John 16:7-11; (c) Rom 10:14-17; cf. Matt 28:18-20; (d) 2 Peter 3:9; Luke 14:26-33; Rom 10:9.

Witnessing through Actions as Well as Words

For those whom we encounter through everyday life, our actions including prayers coupled with our words are important parts of our overall witness for God. Combined effectively, they show people how God's children love both God and them. When someone who is witnessing is able to demonstrate God's love through their *actions as well as their words*, the person being witnessed to will see a fuller picture of God's love than by words alone. Therefore, it is important to witness with both actions and words whenever possible.[a]

Over the years, I have witnessed in many different circumstances including everyday interactions, while traveling, and various forms of ongoing ministry. In some cases when you do not have time to build much of a relationship, it is critically importance to show kindness and genuine concern for the other's well being. Through the Holy Spirit's work, this may be enough to set the stage for successful witnessing where someone listens carefully to what you are saying. While living out your everyday life, you will have opportunities to demonstrate your love and concern for individuals or groups, and some will want to hear what you have to say about God. They will come to understand that God cares about them and that you represent Him. In all cases, if you are able to get individuals to give you the opportunity to discuss God and His desire for them to join His eternal loving righteous family, you are moving in the right direction under the guidance of the Holy Spirit.

Most of you have heard the phrase that "actions speak louder than words." In general, this is true, and it is an important concept for Jesus' followers to remember as they help others get to

---

a: (a) Matt 5:14-16; cf. Eph 2:10; 1 John 3:18.

know God better. I have a friend in ministry in an area of the world where Hindus have controlled much of the population for centuries. Over the years, missionaries had come into his area and had been largely unsuccessful to get others to follow Jesus. They shared the Good News of the One True Creator God in their polytheistic world. They proclaimed a better life now and a perfect life filled with love, joy, and inner peace in the future if people would turn away from their many gods and start following the Son of God, Jesus Christ. After many years of the Church not making any significant progress in this area, my friend was successfully able to help many know God and decide to follow Jesus. It was largely due to the fact that he and his fellow ministers patiently worked with the people of this area helping them *to experience* God's love by helping them with everyday needs including providing clean drinking water, learning personal hygiene, improving education, and helping them find better work as they simultaneously talked to them about the goodness of the One True God versus all of Satan's deceptions that kept them in bondage. As the people saw God's love in action, they were more receptive to hear about how the Creator loves all impartially and wanted them to have a better life now and in the future following Jesus. With God's love being manifested in very tangible ways through Jesus' followers' *actions* along with encouraging them through *God's Word*, many people in this area walked away from Satan's deceptions within Hinduism and a long standing caste system and now live a much more abundant life following Jesus. Let's help others know God using both words *and* actions whenever possible!

Conversational Witnessing

In their book, *Becoming a Contagious Christian*, Bill Hybel, Lee Strobel, Mark Mittelberg discuss how easily Christ's followers can intentionally witness. They state that witnessing should be motivated by love.[(a)] Knowing that God is relational and has created His children to be relational, when we have the opportunity, we should take the time to build relationships looking for opportunities to discuss God's great love and corresponding righteous actions for all. As noted directly above, it is also important to remember that most of the people whom we come in contact with notice what we do as well as what we say. Therefore, it is important to live a loving righteous giving life that accurately expresses God's caring nature.[70]

Later in their book, Hybel, Strobel, and Mittelburg discuss how one should look for ways within everyday conversations to move from the natural to the spiritual. They discuss the idea of looking for ways to build a communication bridge from one to the other within these discussions.[71] In some cases, individuals have already started listening to the Holy Spirit and are eager to discuss God. But normally, you will need to figure out how to transition the conversation from the natural to the spiritual in order to talk about God. It is good somewhere fairly early in a witnessing conversation to come up with a statement or pose a question involving God to see if the other person has any desire to speak about spiritual matters. It could be as simple as saying something like, "I do not know what I would do without God's guidance and help." If the person is receptive, then you will be able to develop a spiritual conversation through God's leading to see how far you should continue the spiritual part of your conversation.

With so many things going on in our lives, the most important part of witnessing is being willing and intentionally open to God's leading at all times throughout each day. *Be intentionally ready to initiate a spiritual conversation!* Then as the Holy Spirit leads, be sensitive to the length and depth of each witnessing encounter. I have had times where I have felt God's leading to

---

a: (a) John 3:16-17; 2 Cor 5:14; 1 John 4:10-19.

speak to someone about Him for only a few minutes, and at other times, I have spoken for hours. God will show you through the other's actions and words how long and on what level you should discuss Him.

From my personal experiences, it has normally been fairly straightforward to start a spiritual discussion based on personal or shared events. In many cases, as you are developing a closer relationship with someone, God will help you make timely transitions from everyday secular conversations into spiritual discussions. As you are developing godly relationships with others, it is also good to introduce them to others who are also followers of Jesus so that they are able to see more clearly what following Jesus might look like. For some, it may be as easy as simply inviting them over to your house to meet some Christian friends or asking them to join you at church, or come to Bible studies, and/or special Christian events.

There are many helpful books and videos available that discuss the various ways to witness *intentionally* to others. A couple additional books to consider are Bill Hybels' *Just Walk Across the Room*, and Dick Innes' *I Hate Witnessing.*[72] If you ask God to help you tell others about Him and His way of life, He will help you witness more effectively taking into consideration everyone's unique personalities and experiences.

Important Words and Concepts

When presenting the Gospel to someone, you should be sensitive to that person's place in their understanding of God. The range can vary significantly from some who are deceived to the point of thinking that there is no Creator to those who know that God exists and loves them deeply, but they do not want to submit to His leadership. When we speak to others about God, we need to remember that everyone is unique. As we follow Jesus, we should be prepared to customize our Gospel presentations including our personal testimony in such a way as to be most effective in reaching each person from their present spiritual thinking.

In any and all cases, there are some basic biblical principles discussed below that everyone should know. Everyone should be ready to discuss the basics of God's freewill Creation and His ongoing redemptive work, which is based on His impartial love and redemptive work that is available to all no matter how bad someone has been. Many of the passages supporting these foundational truths do not need to be memorized, but there are some that you should be familiar with as discussed below.

In most Gospel presentations, it is normally good to start with an overview of God's Creation as described in Genesis chapters one through three. The main purpose of the Creation was to create a freewill holy volunteer family for God. Mankind was created in God's image according to His likeness (Gen 1:26-27) with the ability to obey or disobey Him (Gen 2:16-17). God is ultimately seeking an eternal mutually reciprocating relationship with His mature children. The first couple, Adam and Eve, chose to disobey God (Gen 3:6) separating all humanity for a short time from a close relationship with Him (Gen 3:22-24). With God knowing all things in advance prior to starting the physical part of the Creation, the Father and Son worked out a plan through Jesus' atoning death that would remove all bad actions (sin) from those who would receive Them into their lives as lord and savior (Acts 2:22-39; Rev 13:8; cf. John 3:14-17; Matt 26:36-46). When God finishes adding new members to His eternal holy family, he will finalize His Creation in perfection, which includes a final combined eternal spiritual and physical state (resurrected body) for those who become part of His family (2 Cor 5:21; 1 Peter 2:24; Phil 3:20-21; cf. 1 Thess 4:13-17) and eternal separation from Him for all who do not (2 Peter 3:7; Rev 20:11-15).

The heart of the Gospel message is about how Jesus, the Son of God, the long awaited Anointed One (Messiah), willingly died on a cross suffering shame, excruciating physical pain, and excruciating spiritual pain after taking on sin and being separated for the first time from His perfect unity with the Father making it possible for all who learn to love, trust, and obey God to live eternal sinless lives (Rom 8:28-30; 2 Cor 5:21; 1 Peter 2:24). This incredible miracle came at a great cost to God through the suffering and separation of the Father and Son during the Son's three days in Hades (Sheol) paying the penalty for our sins (separation from His Heavenly Father). The Good News is that although *all* have sinned and fallen short of living in godly perfection (Rom 3:23), everyone of all ages can be made complete with total sin removal by learning to return God's love (1 John 4:10-16), which includes trusting and obeying Him (John 3:16; 36; 14:23; 15:10). With a growing love, trust, and obedience, individuals have a better chance to turn from self-centeredness to God and His way of life (repentance) and ask God to forgive their sins and lead their lives (2 Peter 3:9; Rom 10:4). Once they receive God into their lives as lord and savior, they are brought into His eternal intimate holy family through spiritual birth (John 1:11-13; 3:3, 5; Eph 1:13-14). They become new creations (2 Cor 5:17) gaining the mind of Christ (1 Cor 2:16). Having the mind of Christ and being part of God's eternal close-knit holy family, Jesus' followers joyfully do their part in leading others to God so that as many as possible will receive God into their lives and thereby become part of His eternal holy family (saved) (Matt 28:18-20). Eventually all of trusting children from all time will be in His eternal presence in the New Heaven and on the New Earth living with Him and the other Saints–all in their perfected sinless resurrected bodies (Rev 21:1-6; Phil 3:20-21).

In addition to the Scripture references noted above, there are some important Scripture references shown in *Appendix A* that everyone should be familiar with; they are located immediately after this chapter. Some of the most important Scripture references have asterisks placed in front of them. If you do not have these critical verses memorized, prayerfully consider doing so. Receiving Jesus into one's life is the only way that a person may be perfected and live with God.

If you run across individuals who are not sure about their salvation, ask them if they remember a time when they asked God for forgiveness of their sins and told Him that they would gladly follow Jesus wherever He leads. If the answer is "no," then they need to do so as soon as they are ready. If the answer is "yes," then they should already be new creations and part of God's eternal close-knit holy family.[a] With this being the case, ask if they have noticed a change in their lives since starting to follow Jesus that includes things like wanting to please God;[b] living more loving and righteous lives over time as our Heavenly Father develops them;[c] experiencing a growing concern for others;[d] being happy when someone starts to follow Jesus;[e] and not being afraid of the coming judgment.[f] No one has or will live a perfectly sinless physical life other than Jesus, but everyone who is following Jesus should want to please God and their overall lives should reflect a developing loving righteous walk with God and man.[g] If their answer is "no," then they should seek God's help through prayer and godly action to improve their relationship with Him.

Living Out God's Word and His Leading

It is important that *all* of Jesus' followers continually remain in God's inspired authoritative Word, the Bible, reading and living it out.[h] If they do not, Satan will slowly but surely recondition their minds toward accepting His lies and deceptions.[i]

---

a: (a) Eph 1:13-14; 2 Cor 5:17; (b) John 4:34; (c) Gal 5:18-25; cf. 1 John 3:10, 22; (d) 1 John 4:6-19; cf. Luke 10:27-37; (e) John 15:8-14; 17:13; cf. Luke 15:10; (f) 1 John 4:18; Rev 20:11-15; (g) John 14:23; (h) John 8:31b-32; Rom 12:1-2; (i) John 8:43-44; 2 Cor 11:13-15.

Knowing that Jesus wants all of His followers to become more and more like Him should bring His followers to the place of reading our Heavenly Father's Word on a regular basis and being in touch at all times with Him through ongoing open ended prayer. Prayer should normally be a two way street listening as well as speaking.[a] *Staying in God's Word, praying without ceasing, and keeping an open, obedient mind to God's leading is important for the highest success of Jesus' followers.*

As Jesus' followers study our Heavenly Father's authoritative Word and step out in faith implementing what it says as they follow Jesus' lead through the help of the Holy Spirit, they will come to know more fully our Heavenly Father's will and direction for their lives. It is important when studying God's Word not to misread it by forcing it to say something other than what it meant when it was originally written. There are some who incorrectly try to take what they are reading and subconsciously make it conform to what they have been taught by others or what they prefer it to mean. It is critical for all who want to understand God's Word to allow God to teach them *what He is actually saying* through those who wrote under His inspiration. *It is a common mistake to read into God's Word what we want it to say.* As we discussed earlier (chapter 5), keep in mind the literary and historical context along with grammar as you read through all passages of the Bible and remember that it all fits together without contradictions, if you are understanding it correctly.

As you study God's Word, you may wish to have one or two good literal translations (formal equivalents) such as an English Standard Version (ESV) and/or a New American Standard Bible (NASB) along with one linguistically reconstructed translation (functional equivalent) such as the NIV, which rephrases the original text into wording that is more commonly understood today. Personally, I would avoid the TNIV (Today's

---

a: (a) 2 Thess 5:17.

New International Version) because of its gender leveling, which distorts some of God's Word. The Living translations, sometimes called paraphrased translations, are useful for gaining *overall* perspective, but I do not recommend them for in-depth understanding due to their loss of detail from God's original wording. Keep in mind that the Holy Spirit should be your final guide to proper understanding as you read the translations of your choice and seek truth.[a]

In addition to using a couple good translations, there are many good biblical study aids available such as Bible dictionaries, concordances, and commentaries that are very helpful in understanding the historical, cultural, and religious context along with giving information that was common during ancient biblical times that span several thousand years. But, always keep in mind that commentaries are not God's Word, and therefore be careful not to start trusting any of them as totally factual. There are other books written that may help individuals understand the various literary forms (genres) along with historical and literary contextual fundamentals. One such book is Gordon Fee & Douglas Stuart's *How To Read the Bible for All Its Worth*.[73] It is a practical short guide to general biblical interpretive principles, but it also contains some cultural bias that distorts Scripture. Always ask God to guide your understanding as you read. If we listen to God, He will help us know truth.[b] Part of Jesus' mission was to bear witness to what is real and what is not.[c]

At all times, continue to listen, read, and live out God's Word, the Bible. God speaks mightily to each of His children through His Word and the continual leading of Jesus through the Holy Spirit, who helps us to understand reality and the Father's desire for each of our lives.[d] Listen to your preacher(s), join a local church Bible fellowship and study group, consider other

---

a: (a) 1 John 2:27; cf. 2 Tim 3:16-17; John 8:31b-32; (b) 1 John 2:27; (c) John 18:37; cf. 8:31b-32; (d) Heb 4:12.

Bible studies as led by the Spirit, and most importantly, *do what God tells you through His Word and direct leading.* Many fail to grow in their walk with God simply because they do not implement what He teaches.[a]

Closing Thoughts

Most of us sense that life is something more than a fleeting time on earth prior to death. *That is because life is eternal.* God the Creator, who is eternal, created both the angels and humans as abundant freewill eternal beings. Each has to decide whether or not they want to live with a loving God *under His authority* or be isolated from Him forever.

When we consider the big picture, we want to thank God for His loving kind righteous (holy) nature and creating us to be an intimate part of His eternal holy life. The Father, Son, and Holy Spirit comprise a living "oneness," a godly unity, that is held together with perfect love absent of all sin. There are no divisions within their intimate holy relationship. We were created in God's image according to His likeness to be part of Their intimate holy family and relationship. Through free will, everyone has been marred and everyone's nature struggles with self-centeredness, but God works with all helping those who listen to turn from their self-centered, selfish ways of life to His way of life, which is based on mutual equal love for all. God asks everyone from every generation to turn from self-centeredness and choose eternal life with Him.

God's desire for everyone is to choose good over evil (being hurtful). In one sense, life is simpler than we imagine, because each individual's decision regarding living for self or community determines his or her own eternal destiny. For those

---

a: (a) Heb 5:14.

who choose to receive God as lord and savior, they are choosing good over evil. They are choosing what is good for others *and* for self. For those who choose self *over* others, they are choosing an emptier life that leads to an eternal life of shame, unrest, and suffering.

As each of us journey through this part of eternity, God reveals Himself in a multitude of ways over time wanting all to know Him (spiritual awakenings). To personally know God helps one to submit to His will and confidently follow His lead. Until one knows God and His genuine love for all, it is easier to follow a self-centered path without submitting to Him. But, once an individual has started paying attention to God's revelation of His world and Word, many of Satan's deceptions and his/her own personal self-centered desires become clearer making it much easier to submit to Him. He is a loving holy father and sustainer, who is worthy of respect and honor (reverence).

Can you think of anything more glorious than God and His eternal close-knit holy family? I cannot! What a privilege and honor to be invited into God's holy family to be loved by our Heavenly Father as much as He loves Jesus. What a privilege and honor to be able to join God in the greatest rescue mission of all eternity helping lead people away from Satan's deceptions and hurtful ways into God's marvelous presence and light.

Anyone who stays on life's wide self-centered road without God will miss all of the great opportunities that God has available for everyone. But, if we listen to God and turn to Him, He will start transforming our lives immediately to be more and more like His. We will have the honor and privilege of following Jesus, the promised Messiah, the Son of the Most High, and of experiencing the joy of seeing lives transformed for the better now and forever.

The only way that Jesus' followers can experience the fulness of joy that Jesus experienced at the Cross—and still does as He leads His Church—is to step out into the ongoing spiritual battle and *join God in the greatest rescue mission of all eternity*. Out of a growing genuine love for others, Jesus' followers experience great godly joy by being part of God's holy family and helping rescue those whom they have come to learn to love. *There is no greater joy than leading others to God and seeing them saved from the consequences of unholy living now and in the future with its ultimate disaster of eternal separation from God.*

It is my personal prayer that reading this book has helped you obtain a closer relationship with God as a member of His growing eternal close-knit loving righteous family. If you have not done so yet, it is now time for you to seek God's will in knowing and doing your part in building His eternal holy family. *As you submit more fully to Christ's leadership and His appointed Church leaders, your level of inner peace and joy will continue to grow. As you lead others out of their spiritual darkness*–which has been created by self-centeredness, selfishness, and Satan's deceptions –*into the marvelous light of God's presence, your joy will become more and more like Jesus'*. Keep your eyes fixed on Jesus, the author and perfecter of our faith–who leads all who will follow Him into the Father's preassigned good works for each and eventually into His loving and joyous presence.

If I do not personally meet you on this side of eternity, I want you to know that it is my prayer that you have an exciting and rich life "in Jesus Christ." *As we follow Jesus, let's all thank our Heavenly Father and Jesus for allowing us the honor and privilege of being Their representatives on Earth!*

Appendix: Christ's Followers Proclaim that Jesus Is the Only Way to Eternal Life with God (John 14:6)!

God Is Creating a Close-Knit Eternal Holy Family
With abundant free will came disobedience & sin.
With sin, God's main message to all has been: repent!
(Repent: Turn from self-centeredness to God & His way of life) Matt 3:2; 4:17; Acts 2:38; 2 Peter 3:9

The Crown Jewel of God's Creation!
His Holy Family Being with Him
in the New Heaven & on the New Earth
2 Peter 3:10-13; Rev 21:1-6

Jesus' followers grow in their love, trust, and obedience as they do the good works that have been assigned to them prior to the physical creation of the world (Eph 2:10; cf. Heb 5:14; 10:19-25).

Jesus' atoning death on a cross provides the way (*John 14:6) for all to be with God & one another forever without sin (*2 Cor 5:21; 1 Peter 2:24; cf. Gal 3:13-14; Col 2:13-14) and is available for all who receive Him and His way of life (John 1:11-13; *Rev 3:20; *John 3:16).

God's nature is pure love (1 John 4:10-16) and for those who receive Him, eternal life starts immediately (Eph 1:13-14; 1 John 3:1-3; Phil 3:20-21; Rom 8:14; 1 Cor 5:17) and they undergo God's grace as He develops each of His children to be more and more like Him (Rom 6:22; 8:28-30; cf. John 15: 2; Gal 5:22-23).

If Jesus does not become one's lord and savior, sin separates that one from God, which leads to eternal separation in shame, unrest, and suffering within a place called Hell (*Rom 3:23; *6:23; Rev 20:11-15; cf. Dan 12:2).

Chapter Notes

1. See John 1:11-13 (Rev 3:20); 3:14-17; Rom 8:28-30; Eph 1:13, and others.

2. John 3:3; Greek text: "*gennēthē anōthen.*"

3. Note that during the creation of Adam, he was made in the image according to their likeness. Genesis 1:26 says, "And God said, 'Let Us make Adam in Our image (*betsalmēnû*) according to Our likeness (*kidmûtēnû*).'"

4. When looking at the grammar of the original Greek and many of the English translations of Rom 8:28, it is important to note that the two phrases "to those who love God" and "to those who are called" are in apposition to each other making them an equality. Those who love God *are* those who are called. Secondly, note that those who love God are the same as those who obediently follow Him (John 14:15, 21, 23), and those who love and obey God also learn to trust Him because He is a faithful/trustworthy provider and sustainer (Rom 3:3-4; 1 Cor 1:9; 10:13; 1 Thess 5:24; 2 Tim 2:13; 1 John 4:16). The English words, "believe and trust," are both considered when translating from the same Greek root: *pisteuō*. God provides total sin removal through His Son's atoning death on the Cross (John 3:14-17) for those who learn to trust and obey Him out of love.

5. Consider 1 Cor 9:22; 10:33; James 5:20; & Jude 23.

6. John 18:37-Jesus teaches reality and He is the incarnate Word (*logos*) of God, who lived out God's Word perfectly showing all what godly living looks like (John 1:1-3, 14; 8:28-29; and others).

7. Wikipedia: https://en.wikipedia.org/wiki/Wright_brothers.

8. Consider that each individual was created in Their image according to Their likeness (Our/Us: Gen 1:26). In addition note that the Word, Jesus, was in the presence of His Father at the beginning of the Creation and was of the same nature (essence) as the Father (see the Greek of John 1:1; cf. Heb 1:3). Jesus was always the obedient Son following His Father's will (John 8:28-29; Matt 26:36-39, 42-44; and more) including going to the Cross to remove sin from those who learned to return God's love and obediently follow Him. Jesus' death on the Cross was planned out prior to implementing the physical part of the Creation (Acts 2:22-24; 2 Tim 1:9; 1 Peter 1:18-21; cf. Rev 13:8- grammatical construction shows that the Lamb was slain before the foundation of the world).

9. cf. Rev 12:7; 20:7-10 ; Note: James B. Joseph has translated all Scripture within this book from the original Hebrew (BHS: *Biblia Hebraica Stuttgartensia*-Masoretic Text) and Greek (UBS, Nestle 26) into contemporary English.

10. See Gary Chapman and Arlene Pellican, "Screen Time and Shyness; Screen Time and the Brain," *growing up social* (Chicago: Northfield, 2014).

11. John Ortberg, *When the Game is Over, It All Goes Back in the Box* (Grand Rapids: Zondervan, 2008).

12. Josh McDowell, *A Ready Defense* (San Bernardino: Here's Life, 1990, reprint 1991).

13. C. Mark Corts, *The Truth about Spiritual Warfare: Your Place in the Battle Between God and Satan* (Nashville: Broadman & Holman, 2006).

14. *Geenna* (Gehenna/*gê hinnom*, Valley of Hinnom: Hell). The *Valley of the Sons of Hinnom*, a ravine south of Jerusalem, where some believed that God's final judgment was going to take place (BDAG, 190-91).

15. Compare Matt 25:41; Rev 19:20; 20:10, 14-15. Starting in Isa 14:11, we see a "worm," (in the singular) being used as a covering for those in Sheol. From other Scripture, this would take place in the lower depths of Sheol for the unfaithful. The same words are used in the Hebrew and Greek in Isaiah 66:24 to represent the worm that shall not die for those being tormented forever. God uses the same imagery and wording in Mark 9:43-48 to help all who are listening understand the disgrace and pain of living in Gehenna, in the Kingdom of Hell.

16. Acts 2:27 is a good Scripture to compare to Ps 16:10 in the Greek version of the Old Testament (Septuagint) and the Hebrew version of the Old Testament. Peter is quoting David here and so when we look at Greek and Hebrew versions, we see that those reading the Greek Bible in the first century would have seen the same Greek word that Peter used, *Haidēs*, "Hades," and those reading from the Hebrew Bible would have seen, *Sheolah*, "Sheol," which shows the equivalency of the two words.

17. As noted in endnote #16 directly above, the Old Testament term "Sheol" and the New Testament term "Hades" are referencing the same place, which is a holding place (jail) after Jesus' resurrection for those waiting for the Great White Throne Judgment as described in Rev 20:11-15.

18. Ignatius of Antioch, "To the Trallians," Long Version, Book 2, 2.9.4. This matches Scripture such as Acts 2:27, 31 and Eph 4:8-10.

19. One website shows some of our worlds tallest buildings with the highest in Dubai, UAE (United Arab Emirates) with a height of 2717 ft. finished in 2010, that is a little over one half mile tall (5280 ft./mi.) and the second tallest in Taipei, Taiwan with a height of 1670 ft. finished in 2004, accessed June 26, 2015, URL: http://architecture.about.com/od/skyscrapers/a/Worlds-Tallest-Buildings.htm.

20. Billy Graham, *The Journey: How To Live by Faith in an Uncertain World* (Nashville: W Publishing Group, 2006), has a thought provoking chapter, "Can We Start Over?" Many people have been deceived by Satan into thinking that they cannot start over, but this is one of his many lies. God desires all to turn to Him and be saved (John 3:16; 2 Peter 3:9).

21. Acts 2:22-24; cf. Rev 13:8-see the Greek for grammatical arrangement and note that Jesus' death on the Cross was arranged prior to the Creation being implemented physically; cf. 1 Peter 1:18-21; 2 Tim 1:9. God teaches us through His Word that sin causes chaos and great pain, which will eventually turn into great joy throughout the physical and spiritual world for those who listen to Him (Rom 8:18-23; Rom 6:23; Rev 21:1-4).

22. Matt 22:14, *polloi gar eisin klētoi, oligoi de eklectoi,* "for many are called, but few are chosen."

23. In his letter to the Roman (8:28-30), Paul states that those who love God (grammatical apposition to "called") are the called (*klētois*), and have also been predestined (*proorizō*) to be made righteous and glorified.

24. My translation of the Greek for Luke 14:26 using present day wording is, "If someone comes to me and does not *regard less* his father and mother and wife and children and brothers and sisters and even his own life, he is not able to be my disciple (follower)."

25. Billy Graham, *How To Be Born Again* (Waco: Word Books, 1977), 152-53.

26. Greg E. Viehman, M.D., *The God Diagnosis: a Physician's Shocking Journey to Life after Death* (Sylacauga, AL: Big Mac Publishers, 2010), 11-15.

27. "And we know that for those who are loving God, He works all things for good, for those being called according to (His) predetermined plan (*prothesin*); for whom He foreknew (*proegnō*), indeed He predestined (*proōrisen*) to be conformed together (*summorphous*) into the image (*eikonos*) of His Son for Him to be the first (*prōtotokon*) with (*en*) many brothers (*adelphois*); and whom He predestined, these indeed He called, and those whom He called, these indeed He justified (*edikaiōsen*); and those whom He justified, these indeed He glorified (*edoxasen*) [Romans 8:28-30])." Note that those who love God are those who are predestined to be called. In the Greek grammar, the second participial phrase is considered in apposition with the first making them equal: "And we know that *for those who are loving God*, He works all things for good, *for those being called* according to (His) predetermined plan." The range of meaning for *eikonos,* is "image, form, appearance, an object resembles or has been shaped to resemble the form or appearance of something else" (BDAG, 281-82); this is the same Greek word used in the Septuagint to describe God's creation of man (Gen 1:26), "according to our image and likeness."

28. In many places within Scripture, the translators translate some form of the Greek root *pisteuō*, "to believe, to trust" simply as "believe," which does not cover properly the Greek idea of knowing and trusting- having confidence in. In John 3:15 and 3:16, John used a present tense Greek participle in his Gospel message showing **present ongoing belief and trust**: "trusting." God's salvation was for all within the World who would learn to trust Him on an ongoing basis. Trust and obey, there is no other Way (John 3:14-17, 36). Some form of the root of the noun *pistis*, "faith, trust, belief," is used consistently throughout the New Testament to indicate both trust and belief simultaneously and many times is translated into words such as "faithful, trustworthy."

29. "And God said, 'Let us make Adam in our image (*be-tsalmē-nū*) according to our likeness (*ki-demūtē-nū*) . . . , ' And God created the man Adam in His image, in the image of God He created him, male and female He created them [cf. Rom 2:11-16]."

30. In Galatians 3:28, looking at the Greek wording *arsen kai thēlu*, "male and female" compared to this same wording in the Greek Septuagint (Gen 1:27; cf. 2:2:24) and Greek New Testament (Matt 19:4-5) as referring to "husband and wife" within a marriage, one notes within the context of the passage and the Bible as a whole that this wording is referring to marriages and the husband's headship over his wife, which no longer exists in heaven-all are equal.

31. In verses 21 and 23, John completes each verse with a *hina* clause indicating a probable outcome within the world with the Church showing godly unity vs. a purpose of that unity: the World will know that the Father sent Him, and that the Father loves those born again spiritually just as He loves Jesus. See BDAG, page 477, which discusses the *hina* marker used for results vs. purpose depending on context.

32. Regarding the idea of aorist constructions used to represent ongoing action without emphasis on beginning or end (timeless; Gnomic), see A.T. Robertson, *A Grammar of the Green New Testament in the Light of Historical Research,* 3rd ed, reprint 1934, page 836 f.

33. The Creation glorifies God (1 Chronicles 16:23, 31–31) and is filled with knowledge of God's glory (Habakkuk 2:14). God's glory can be seen through His Creation (Psalm 19:1, 29; 96:11–13; 97:6; Isaiah 6:3) especially through those who are called by His name whom He has created, shaped, and worked with. In the Greek Septuagint, God's Word says that "in my glory" I have prepared, molded, and worked with him, the one who is called for my purposes. In Romans 11:36, God speaks through Paul saying "all things have come forth from Him and exist through Him and (therefore) belong to Him. Paul goes on to say, "to Him is the glory into the ages (for ever)," meaning that God's glory can be seen in everything that exists. We have a song that teaches this doctrine titled "To God Be the Glory." It starts with this thought, "To God be the glory—great things He has done! So loved He the world that He gave us His son." God's

people are to declare His glory: 1 Chronicles 16:7–36; Psalm 96:3–10; 105:1–15 ascribing to Him the glory that is due Him: Psalm 29:1–2; 96:7–10.

34. For additional reading regarding the sharing of Jesus' glory with all Believers, see James B. Joseph, *Unity and Obedient Discipleship in John 17* (Saarbrücken: LAMBERT Academic Publishing, 2016) and *Victory in Jesus: Being a Child of God* (Kings Mountain: Drawbridge Publishing, 1997).

35. Gen 2:24b (Hebrew): "and he shall cling (hold onto) to his wife and they shall become 'one' flesh" (close unity); Greek Septuagint: and the two shall become 'one' flesh (close unity); and Greek New Testament: Matt 19:5: "and the two shall become 'one' flesh" (close unity).

36. Judges 20:11 (Hebrew language): "Every man of Israel gathered to the city uniting 'as one' man" (close unity); Greek Septuagint: "Every man of Israel gathered together into the city 'as one' man" (close unity). Cf. Judges 20:1, 8.

1 Sam 11:7 (Hebrew language): "And the dread/awe (BDB, 808) of YHWH fell upon the people and they came out 'as one man'" (close unity). Greek Septuagint: "as one man" (close unity).

37. Constantine Scouteris, "The People of God-Its Unity and Its Glory: A Discussion of John 17:17-24 in the Light of Patristic Thought," *The Greek Orthodox Theological Review* 30, no. 4 (Winter 1985): 399-414.

38. Scouteris, "The People of God," 401-01.

39. Scouteris, "The People of God," 403.

40. Scouteris, "The People of God," 405-06.

41. Scouteris, "The People of God," 407.

42. Scouteris, "The People of God," 411.

43. Scouteris, "The People of God," 414.

44. C. H. Dodd, *The Interpretation of the Fourth Gospel* (New York: Cambridge University Press, 1953, reprint 1958), 187-200; cf. John 14:20.

45. Dodd, *Interpretation of the Fourth Gospel,* 196

46. Dodd, *Interpretations of the Fourth Gospel,* 197

47. Consider Isaiah who after seeing God's holiness, which is based on His pure loving righteous nature, and then recognizing his own sinful fallen nature turned to God for help. After God removed his sin, Isaiah immediately wanted to do God's will not knowing or caring that he was volunteering for a very difficult assignment as a prophet of God proclaiming imminent upcoming destruction for his countrymen (Isa 6:1-13).

48. Billy Graham, *Just As I Am: the Autobiography of Billy Graham* (New York: Harper Collins, 1997), 26-27.

49. Graham, *Just As I Am*, 28.

50. Graham, *Just As I Am,* 29-30.

51. Graham, *Just As I Am,* 30.

52. Bush, *Decision Points*, 31.

53. Bush, *Decision Points*, 30.

54. James M. Boice, *Christ's Call to Discipleship* (Minneapolis: Grason, 1986), 139.

55. Boice, *Christ's Call to Discipleship*, 35.

56. Kyle Idleman, *Not a Fan: Becoming a Completely Committed Follower of Jesus* (Grand Rapids: Zondervan, 2011), 11-13.

57. Kyle, *Not a Fan*, 14-15.

58. Kyle, *Not a Fan*, 158-61.

59. James B. Joseph, *No More Walls! Creation of One New Man in Christ: Ephesians 2:11-22* (Saarbrücken: LAMBERT Academic Publishing, 2015), 25-62.

60. Billy Graham, *The Journey*, 62.

61. Josh McDowell and Bob Hostetler, *Beyond Belief to Convictions* (Carol Stream: Tyndale House, 2002), 296.

62. Graham, *The Journey*, 74-76.

63. Graham, *The Journey*, 77-78. For a practical introduction to discipleship, consider working through Henry Blackaby's 13 week course, *Experiencing God*, rev. ed. (Nashville: Broadman and Holman, 2008).

64. Dietrich Bonhoeffer, *Letters & Papers from Prison*, rev. ed., ed. Eberhard Bethge (New York: Simon & Schuster, 1997), 411.

65. Dietrich Bonhoeffer, *The Cost of Discipleship* (New York: Touchstone, 1995).

66. Bonhoeffer, *Letters and Papers from Prison*, 369-70.

67. Max Lucado, *Out Live Your Life* (Nashville: Thomas Nelson, 2010).

68. See James B. Joseph, *No More Walls!*, for a detailed breakdown of this passage.

69. Flavius Claudius Iulianus (Julian), *Against the Galilaeans,* in *The Works of the Emperor Julian,* vol. 3, lines 166-238 and other pages; Loeb Classical Library (Cambridge: Harvard University Press, 1923; reprint 1998).

70. Bill Hybels and Mark Mittleburg, *Becoming a Contagious Christian* (Grand Rapids: Zondervan, 1994), 67ff.

71. Hybels and Mittleburg, *Becoming a Contagious Christian*, 135ff.

72. Bill Hybels, *Just Walk Across the Room: Simple Steps Pointing People to Faith* (Grand Rapids: Zondervan, 2006);
    Dick Innes, *I Hate Witnessing: A Handbook for Effective Christian Communications.* rev. ed. (San Clemente: Acts Communications, 2003).

73. Gordon D. Fee and Douglas Stuart, *How To Read the Bible for All Its Worth*, 4th ed. (Grand Rapids: Zondervan, 2014).

Bibliography

Bibles: Primary Sources

Biblia Hebraica Stuttgartensia. 3d ed. Stuttgart: Deutsche
Bibelgesellschaft, 1987.

The Greek New Testament. 3d UBS ed. Stuttgart: Biblia-Druck,
1988.

The Septuagint with Apocrypha: Greek and English. London:
Samuel Bagster & Sons, 1851. Reprint, Peabody:
Hendrickson, 2001.

Biblical References

Bauer, Walter. *A Greek-English Lexicon of the New Testament and
other Early Christian Literature.* Rev. and ed. Frederick W.
Danker. 3d ed. Chicago: The University of Chicago Press,
2000.

Brown, Francis, S. R Driver, and Charles A. Briggs. *The New
Brown-Driver-Briggs-Gesenius Hebrew-English Lexicon.*
Peabody: Hendrickson, 1979.

Kohlenberger III, John R., Edward W. Goodrick, and James A.
Swanson. *The Exhaustive Concordance to the Greek New
Testament.* Grand Rapids: Zondervan, 1995.

Liddell, Henry George and Robert Scott. *A Greek-English
Lexicon.* Rev. & augmented by Henry Stuart Jones and
Roderick McKenzie. 9th ed. Oxford: Oxford University
Press, 1940. Reprint, 1990.

Robertson, A. T. *A Grammar of the Green New Testament in the Light of Historical Research,* 3rd ed. NY: Hodder & Stoughton, 1919. Reprint, Nashville: Broadman, 1934.

General References

Blackaby, Henry. *Experiencing God.* Rev. ed. Nashville: Broadman and Holman, 2008.

Boice, James M. *Christ's Call to Discipleship.* Minneapolis: Grason, 1986.

Bonhoeffer, Dietrich. *The Cost of Discipleship.* New York: Touchstone, 1995.

_____. *Letters & Papers from Prison.* Rev. ed. New York: Simon & Schuster, 1997.

Bush, George W. *Decision Points.* New York: Crown, 2010.

Chan, Francis and Preston Sprinkle. *Erasing Hell: What God Said about Eternity, and the Things That We Have Made Up.* Colorado Springs: David C Cook, 2011.

Chapman, Gary and Arlene Pellican. *growing up social.* Chicago: Northfield, 2014.

Corts, Mark C. *The Truth about Spiritual Warfare: Your Place in the Battle between God and Satan.* Nashville: Broadman & Holman, 2006.

Dodd, C. H. *The Interpretation of the Fourth Gospel.* New York: Cambridge University Press, 1953. Reprint, 1958.

Fee, Gordon D. and Douglas Stuart. *How To Read the Bible for All Its Worth.* 4th ed. Grand Rapids: Zondervan, 2014.

Graham, Billy. *How To Be Born Again.* Waco: Word Books, 1977.

_____. *The Journey: How To Live by Faith in an Uncertain World.* Nashville: W Publishing, 2006.

_____. *Just as I Am: The Autobiography of Billy Graham.* New York: Harper Collins, 1997.

Hybels, Bill. *Just Walk Across the Room: Simple Steps Pointing People to Faith.* Grand Rapids: Zondervan, 2004.

Hybels, Bill, Lee Strobel, and Mark Mittleburg. *Becoming a Contagious Christian.* Grand Rapids: Zondervan, 1994.

Idleman, Kyle. *Not a Fan: Becoming a Completely Committed Follower of Jesus.* Grand Rapids: Zondervan, 2011.

Innes, Dick. *I Hate Witnessing: A Handbook for Effective Christian Communications.* Rev. ed. San Clemente: Acts Communications, 2003.

Iulianus (Julian), Flavius Claudius. *Against the Galilaeans.* In *The Works of the Emperor Julian,* vol. 3. Loeb Classical Library. Translated by Wilmer Cave Wright. Cambridge: Harvard University Press, 1923. Reprint, 1998.

Joseph, James B. *Experiencing Jesus' Joy*. Lynchburg: Liberty University Press, 2013.

_____. *Experiencing Jesus Joy through Obedient Discipleship*. Winston-Salem, NC: IJS Publishing, 2016.

_____. *No More Walls! Creation of One New Man in Christ: Ephesians 2:11-22*. Saarbrücken: LAMBERT Academic Publishing, 2015.

_____. *Unity and Obedient Discipleship in John 17*. Saarbrücken: LAMBERT Academic Publishing, 2016.

_____. *Victory in Jesus: Being a Child of God*. Kings Mountain: Drawbridge Publishing, 1997.

Lucado, Max. *Out Live Your Life: You Were Made To Make a Difference*. Nashville: Thomas Nelson, 2010.

McDowell, Josh. *A Ready Defense*. San Bernardino: Here's Life, 1990. Reprint, 1991.

McDowell, Josh and Bob Hostetler. *Beyond Belief to Conversion*. Carol Stream: Tyndale House, 2002.

Metzger, Bruce M. *The Canon of the New Testament: Its Origin, Development, and Significance*. New York: Oxford University Press, 1997.

Milne, Bruce. *The Message of John*. Downers Grove: InterVarsity, 1993.

Ortberg, John. *When the Game Is Over, It All Goes Back in the Box.* Grand Rapids: Zondervan, 2008.

Piper, John. *What Jesus Demands from the World.* Wheaton: Crossway, 2006.

Scouteris, Constantine. "The People of God–Its Unity and Its Glory: A Discussion of John 17:17-24 in Light of Patristic Thought." *The Greek Orthodox Theological Review* 30, no. 4 (Winter 1985): 399-414.

Stott, John. *Basic Christianity.* 2nd ed. London: InterVarsity, 1971.

Viehman, Greg E., M.D. *The God Diagnosis: a Physician's Shocking Journey to Life after Death.* Sylcauga, AL: Big Mac Publishers, 2010.

Made in the USA
Middletown, DE
19 July 2023

34984349R00126